Rigor Made Easy

Getting Started

Barbara R. Blackburn

Routledge
Taylor & Francis Group
New York London

First published 2012 by Eye On Education

Published 2013 by Routledge
711 Third Avenue, New York, NY 10017, USA
2 Park Square, Milton Park, Abingdon, Oxon OX14 4RN

Routledge is an imprint of the Taylor & Francis Group, an informa business

Library of Congress Cataloging-in-Publication Data
Blackburn, Barbara R., 1961–
Rigor made easy : getting started / Barbara R. Blackburn.
        p.   cm.
ISBN 978-1-59667-215-4
1. School improvement programs.
2. Educational leadership.
3. Classroom environment.
4. Academic achievement.
I. Title.
LB2822.8.B53 2012
371.2'07—dc23   2011052319
10 9 8 7 6 5 4 3 2

ISBN: 978-1-596-67215-4 (pbk)
Cover Designer: Dave Strauss, 3FoldDesign

Also by Barbara R. Blackburn

Rigor Is NOT a Four-Letter Word

Rigor in Your School:
A Toolkit for Leaders
(with Ronald Williamson)

Rigorous Schools and Classrooms:
Leading the Way
(with Ronald Williamson)

Classroom Motivation from A to Z:
How to Engage Your Students in Learning

Classroom Instruction from A to Z:
How to Promote Student Learning

Literacy from A to Z

The Principalship from A to Z
(with Ronald Williamson)

Also Available from Eye On Education

Critical Thinking and Formative Assessments:
Increasing the Rigor in Your Classroom
Betsy Moore and Todd Stanley

Students Taking Charge:
Inside the Learner-Active, Technology-Infused Classroom
Nancy Sulla

Differentiation Is an Expectation:
A School Leader's Guide to Building
a Culture of Differentiation
Kimberly Kappler Hewitt and Daniel K. Weckstein

Teaching Critical Thinking:
Using Seminars for 21st Century Literacy
Terry Roberts and Laura Billings

Math in Plain English:
Literacy Strategies for the Mathematics Classroom
Amy Benjamin

Differentiating by Readiness:
Strategies and Lesson Plans for Tiered
Instruction, Grades K–8
Joni Turville, Linda Allen, and Leann Nickelsen

Active Literacy Across the Curriculum
Heidi Hayes Jacobs

Battling Boredom:
99 Strategies to Spark Student Engagement
Bryan Harris

Writer's Workshop for the Common Core:
A Step-by-Step Guide
Warren E. Combs

Rigor Made Easy is dedicated to my mother.
Her work as a school secretary taught me the importance
of all the stakeholders in the school.
She has always inspired me, been patient with me,
and loved me unconditionally.
I would not be who I am today without her.

About the Author

Dr. Barbara Blackburn has dedicated her life to raising the level of rigor and motivation for professional educators and students alike. What differentiates Barbara's 12 books are her easily executable, concrete examples based on decades of experience as a teacher, professor, and consultant. Barbara's dedication to education was inspired in her early years by her parents, Bob and Rose. Her father's doctorate and lifetime career as a professor taught her the importance of professional training. Her mother's career as a school secretary shaped Barbara's appreciation of the effort all staff play in the education of every child.

Barbara has taught early childhood, elementary, middle, and high school students and has served as an educational consultant for three publishing companies. She holds a master's degree in school administration and is certified as a teacher and a school principal in North Carolina. She received her Ph.D. from the University of North Carolina at Greensboro. In 2006, she received the award for Outstanding Junior Professor at Winthrop University. She recently left her position at the University of North Carolina at Charlotte to write and speak full time.

In addition to speaking at state and national conferences, she also regularly presents workshops for teachers and administrators in elementary, middle, and high schools. Her workshops are lively and engaging and filled with practical information. She can be reached through her Web site, www.barbarablackburnonline.com.

Acknowledgments

Writing a book is never an easy process, nor is it an isolated one. I particularly appreciate:

My husband and stepson who give me the time to write,
My mother, father, and sisters who encourage and support me,
My best friend Abbigail, who listens, advises, and laughs
    with me.

To the people at Eye On Education who make all my work
    possible, thank you.
Bob Sickles, who provides the foundation for all my work,
Heather and Michele, who streamline almost everything
    for me,
Lauren Davis, my editor, who was instrumental in my revisions to the manuscript,
Morgan Dubin, who taught me what I know about social
    media, so I could connect with more teachers,
Dave Strauss, who always designs the perfect cover,
Matthew Williams, who provided a new layout design to
    facilitate reading.

For those who reviewed the draft, your feedback was critical to the final product.

Patricia Conner, Berryville Public School District, Berryville, AR
Rose Colby, Consultant, Epping, NH
Carolyn Guthrie, Miami-Dade County Schools, FL
Paul Hankins, Silver Creek High School, Sellersburg, IN
Ann Linson, East Noble School Corporation, Kendallville, IN
Eric Williams, York County Schools, Yorktown, VA

Finally, to those teachers and leaders whom I meet during my workshops, through my newsletter and blog, and through social media, you inspire me every day to remember the power of individuals to make a difference with students. I want to particularly thank the educators in Chicago Area 10, Calcasieu Parish, Louisiana, Pasadena Independent School District, and AdvancEd and their conference participants in Wyoming.

Contents

Free Downloads

Many of the tools discussed and displayed in this book are also available on the Routledge website as Adobe Acrobat files. Permission has been granted to purchasers of this book to download these tools and print them.

You can access these downloads by visiting www.routledge.com/9781596672154 and click on the Free Downloads tab.

Bonus Templates

Rigor Definition and Myths Bookmark
Tic-Tac-Toe Chart
Points to Ponder Reflection Sheet
Study Guide for Teachers
Study Guide for Leaders

Introduction

You might have picked up this book, looked at the title, and thought, "Rigor Made Easy? She's got to be joking." I understand, because I work with teachers all over the nation who feel that way. Notice I didn't say rigor *is* easy, I said it's *made* easy.

Too often, rigor has become teaching a rigid curriculum, preparing for a standardized test, planning lessons that match a certain format, or teaching to a particular evaluation criteria. Some of those may include aspects of rigor, but I believe true rigor is infused throughout all aspects of the classroom.

Rigor is more than staying inside a certain box or labeling a class. Rigor includes creating lessons and activities that are challenging for all students. It also includes other characteristics, listed below using the acronym EASY:

⇨ Rigor Made EASY

Engages all students
Accommodates all learners
Scaffolds learning
Yields results

This book, my fourth on rigor, is an introduction to rigor. *Rigor Is NOT a Four-Letter Word*, which was my first book on rigor, was designed for those looking for classroom-based ideas. Here, we'll revisit some of those activities and look at new ones, all through an expanded lens of kindergarten through twelfth grade. You'll also find activities that apply to any subject area, that include technology as an option, and that are applicable in a classroom using differentiated instruction.

If you are looking for leadership strategies for schools or districts, please take a look at *Rigorous Schools and Classrooms: Leading the Way* and *Rigor in Your School: A Toolkit for Leaders*, both cowritten with Ron Williamson.

Before you begin, I'd like to tell you a bit about my beliefs, which are shaped by my parents. My mother was a school secretary and modeled for me the important role of everyone in the school. My father was a teacher, coach, and college professor, who has now retired "for the third time" and shows me every day the value of lifelong learning. I would never have become a teacher without them.

⇨ Barbara's Beliefs

> The individual teacher has power.
> Students reflect teachers' expectations.
> All students can learn.
> Teachers should focus on what they can control.

First, I have seen the power of an individual classroom teacher. My most memorable teachers were also the ones who held me to high standards. As I work with schools, I am privileged to see teachers who make a difference, even in difficult circumstances. One teacher always has made a difference in the life of a student. One teacher always will make a difference in the life of a student.

Next, I know that students reflect our perspective of them. When we have high expectations and provide support, students will rise to new levels of learning. And when we think they can't learn, they don't. It really is that basic.

In order to have high expectations, we must believe that all students can learn. We all say we believe that, but those beliefs must be so deep that we never give up on a student. As Richard Dufour says, "Don't tell me you believe all children can learn;

tell me what you do when they don't" (Dufour, 2006). In other words, back up your words with actions.

Finally, we should focus on the things we can control and quit worrying about those things that are out of our control. With every chapter, I asked myself, "Is this something a teacher could decide to implement in his or her classroom?" I often meet teachers who believe they have no control over anything, especially when they are required to use scripted programs. But that's not true. At the very least, we control our attitude. When we focus on what we can control, we feel more productive.

I hope you enjoy and learn from *Rigor Made Easy*. We'll look at what rigor is and how it looks in a classroom. Then we'll jump into five chapters of strategies, some with a technology basis, some without. With the variety, every teacher can find activities that will work in his or her classroom.

Information about the Common Core State Standards, differentiated instruction, student motivation, and engagement are embedded throughout those chapters. Last, we'll discuss a few challenges you may face.

Keep in mind that increasing rigor in your classroom can be made EASY, and it is manageable if you take it one step at a time. I'm here to facilitate the process, and I've provided tools you can use to reflect on your learning. Enjoy the journey!

⇨ *Rigor Made EASY*

Engages all students
Accommodates all learners
Scaffolds learning
Yields results

1

Understanding Rigor

Rigor is creating an environment in which each student is expected to learn at high levels, each student is supported so he or she can learn at high levels, and each student demonstrates learning at high levels (Blackburn, 2008).

When I am in schools working with teachers, they are quick to tell me they care about rigor because they are told they have to. Then they ask me why I care about rigor. My response is simple. There are other reasons, such as the clear research base that shows students need more rigor, the new Common Core State Standards (CCSS) that require more rigor, or the number of students who graduate from high school ill-prepared for college or the workforce. But my most important reason is this: rigor is about helping students learn at higher levels, and that's why I became a teacher.

I was reminded of this a few years ago when I was in a school and met Gabrielle. My favorite question to ask students is, "If you were in charge of the school, what would you change?" Her answer was insightful. She said, "For people who don't understand as much . . . [they should] be in higher level classes to understand more [because] if they already don't know much, you don't want to teach them to not know much over and over." Now, you might laugh at her comment, but it is very true. Many students aren't really growing; they are learning the same things, or they are not learning at all. My passion for rigor comes from my teacher's heart: I want each student to have the opportunity to learn and grow.

Myths About Rigor

Before we look at what rigor is, let's take a moment to look at the myths that distract from true rigor.

⇾ Five Myths About Rigor

1. Lots of homework is a sign of rigor.
2. Rigor means doing more.
3. Rigor is not for everyone.
4. Providing support means lessening rigor.
5. Resources equal rigor.

Myth #1: Lots of Homework Is a Sign of Rigor

For many people, the best indicator of rigor is the amount of homework required of students. Some teachers pride themselves on the amount of homework they assign, and there are parents who judge teachers by homework quantity.

Realistically, all homework is not equally useful. Some of it is just busywork, assigned by teachers because principals or parents expect it. One study (Wasserstein, 1995) found that students described busywork as unimportant and, therefore, not satisfying. Contrary to what many adults believe, students viewed hard work as important, and they enjoyed the challenge and enjoyment that went with accomplishing a task that was hard.

For some students, doing a higher quantity of homework leads to burnout. When that occurs, students are less likely to complete homework and may be discouraged about any learning activity.

"Doing more" often means doing more low-level activities, frequently repetitions of things already learned. Such narrow and rigid approaches to learning do not define a rigorous classroom. Students learn in many different ways. Just as instruction must vary to meet the individual needs of students, so must homework. Rigorous and challenging learning experiences will vary with the student. Their designs will vary, as will their duration. Ultimately, it is the quality of the assignment that makes a difference in terms of rigor.

Myth #2: Rigor Means Doing More

Many parents and educators believe that a rigorous classroom is characterized by requiring students to do more than they currently do, and that rigor is defined by the content of a lesson, the number of problems assigned, the amount of reading, or the number of requirements.

True rigor is expecting every student to learn and perform at high levels. This requires instruction that allows students to delve deeply into their learning, to engage in critical thinking and problem solving activities, to be curious and imaginative, and to demonstrate agility and adaptability (Wagner, 2008a). Simply put, more is not necessarily better, especially when more is low-level or repetitive.

Myth #3: Rigor Is Not for Everyone

Some teachers think the only way to assure success for everyone is to lower standards and lessen rigor. This may mask a hidden belief that some students can't really learn at high levels. You may have heard of the Pygmalion Effect: students live up to or down to our expectations of them.

I was recently working with a school that had one solution for increasing rigor—put all students in advanced classes. That may be an option, but I'm not convinced that it is the best way to increase rigor. First, not all students are ready for an advanced class without extra support. Second, that choice sends the message that the only teachers capable of rigorous instruction are those who teach advanced students. I know from my own experience as a teacher of struggling students reading far below their grade level that any teacher can be rigorous, and any student can reach higher levels with the right support.

Myth #4: Providing Support Means Lessening Rigor

In the United States, we believe in rugged individualism. We are to pull ourselves up by our bootstraps and do things on our own. Working in teams or accepting help is often seen as a sign of weakness.

Supporting students so they can learn at high levels is central to the definition of rigor. As teachers design lessons that move students toward more challenging work, they must provide scaffolding to support them as they learn.

Ron Williamson, my coauthor on my leadership books, asked teachers and parents about their experience with rigor. Both groups repeatedly told stories of how successful they were on rigorous tasks when they felt a high level of support, a safety net. Often, people described tasks that were initially not successful. Only after additional time or effort did they experience success. In fact, many people said they would not have been successful without strong support.

The same is true for students. They are motivated to do well when they value what they are doing, and when they believe that they have a chance of success. The most successful classrooms and schools are those that build a culture of success, celebrate success, and create a success mentality.

Myth #5: Resources Equal Rigor

Another common refrain is "If we bought this program or textbook or technology, then we would be rigorous." I've worked for two textbook companies and one instructional technology company, and I learned a critical lesson: it's never the resources; it's always how you use them. Mediocre materials in the hands of a great teacher are effective. Excellent materials used by a poor teacher provide minimal results. And excellent materials with an excellent teacher can work wonders.

The right resources can certainly help increase the rigor in your classroom. However, raising the level of rigor for your students is not dependent on the resources you have.

Defining Rigor

My definition of rigor has a sharp focus on instruction: creating an environment in which

- ◆ each student is expected to learn at high levels,
- ◆ each student is supported so he or she can learn at high levels, and
- ◆ each student demonstrates learning at high levels.

Notice we are looking at the environment you create. The tri-fold approach to rigor is not limited to the curriculum students are expected to learn. It is more than a specific lesson or instructional strategy. It is deeper than what a student says or does in response to a lesson. True rigor is the result of weaving together all elements of schooling to raise students to higher levels of learning. Let's take a deeper look at the three aspects of the definition.

Expecting Students to Learn at High Levels

The first component of rigor is creating an environment in which each student is expected to learn at high levels. Having high expectations starts with the recognition that every student possesses the potential to be his or her best, no matter what.

Almost every teacher or leader I talk with says, "We have high expectations for our students." Sometimes that is evidenced by the behaviors in the school; at other times, actions don't match the words. There are concrete ways to implement and assess rigor in classrooms.

As you design lessons that incorporate more rigorous opportunities for learning, you will want to consider the questions that are embedded in the instruction. Higher-level questioning is an integral part of a rigorous classroom. Look for open-ended questions, ones that are at the higher levels of Bloom's Taxonomy (analysis, synthesis). You'll find more on questioning in Chapter 3: Increase Complexity.

It is also important to pay attention to how you respond to student questions. When I visit schools, it is not uncommon to see teachers who ask higher-level questions. But I then see some of the same teachers accept low-level responses from students. In rigorous classrooms, teachers push students to respond at high levels. They ask extending questions. If a student does not know the answer, the teacher continues to probe and guide the student to an appropriate answer, rather than moving on to the next student.

Supporting Students to Learn at High Levels

High expectations are important, but the most rigorous schools assure that each student is supported so he or she can learn at high levels, which is the second part of our definition. It is essential that teachers design lessons that move students to more challenging work while simultaneously providing ongoing scaffolding to support students' learning as they move to those higher levels.

Providing additional scaffolding throughout lessons is one of the most important ways to support students. This can occur in a variety of ways, but it requires that teachers ask themselves during every step of their lessons, "What extra support might my students need?" In Chapter 4: Give Appropriate Support and Guidance, we'll explore this is more detail.

⇨ *Examples of Scaffolding Strategies*

♦ Asking guiding questions
♦ Chunking information
♦ Color-coding steps in a project
♦ Writing standards as questions for students to answer
♦ Using visuals and graphic organizers such as a math graphic organizer for word problems, interactive reading guides, and other tools

Ensuring Students Demonstrate Learning at High Levels

The third component of a rigorous classroom is providing each student with opportunities to demonstrate learning at high levels. A teacher recently said to me, "If we provide more challenging lessons that include extra support, then learning will happen." What I've learned is that if we want students to show us they understand what they learned at a high level, we also need to provide opportunities for students to demonstrate they have truly mastered that learning. One way to accomplish that is through increased student engagement.

Student engagement is a critical aspect of rigor. In too many classrooms, most of the instruction consists of the teacher-centered, large-group instruction, perhaps in an interactive lecture or discussion format. The general practice during these lessons is for the teacher to ask a question and then call on a student to respond. While this provides an opportunity for one student to demonstrate understanding, the remaining students don't do so.

Another option would be for the teacher to allow all students to pair-share, respond with thumbs up or down, write their answers on small whiteboards and share their responses, or respond on handheld computers that tally the responses. Such activities hold each student accountable for demonstrating his or her understanding. We'll explore this concept in Chapter 6: Raise Expectations.

⇒ *Indicators of High Levels of Student Engagement*

Negative Indicators	Positive Indicators
◆ One student responds.	◆ All students respond.
◆ Two or three students discuss content.	◆ All students discuss content in small groups.
◆ Students are asked if they understand with a simple yes or no and no probing.	◆ All students write a response in a journal or on an exit slip.

If this seems a bit overwhelming, remember that creating a more rigorous classroom is a journey, one that continues as you and your students learn and grow and change. The next five chapters will provide a variety of activities you can use or adapt immediately, no matter what grade level and/or subject you teach. Please remember that there is no magic formula for increasing rigor. It's a process of continually adjusting your expectations, instruction, and assessments to ensure that each of your students learns at higher and higher levels.

I know you will be successful in your journey. The fact that you are reading this book means you continue to learn, and that is at the heart of rigor. Expect the best, understand you won't be perfect, and know that in the end, you will have made a difference to students.

The table on the next page provides a breakdown of the strategies you'll learn in the next chapters.

⇨ *Strategies to Increase Rigor*

Chapter 2: Raise the Level of Content	The Common Core State Standards Selecting Appropriate Texts Multiple Sources of Information Depth, Not Coverage
Chapter 3: Increase Complexity	Digging Deeper Quality Questions Ratchet Up Reviews Take It Up a Notch
Chapter 4: Give Appropriate Support and Guidance	Modeling Gradual Release Working With Struggling Learners Extra Help and Support
Chapter 5: Open Your Focus	Begin With Discovery Choices Perspectives Connections
Chapter 6: Raise Expectations	Student Motivation Beliefs and Actions Ensuring Rigor for EACH Student Celebrating Progress

2

Raise the Level of Content

Raising the level of content you teach is our first broad strategy to increase rigor in the classroom.

Raise the Level of Content

The Common Core State Standards
Selecting Appropriate Texts
Multiple Sources of Information
Depth, Not Coverage

The Common Core State Standards

At the heart of the new Common Core State Standards is a focus on higher expectations. One of the major reasons for a push for the standards was the lack of rigor in many schools today, and the need to better prepare students for college and the workforce.

Developed in a climate of conflicting definitions and perceptions of rigor, the CCSS succeeded in providing a well-defined set of expectations for each grade level in the areas of reading/language arts and math. According to the Fordham Institute's study, *The State of State Standards* (July 2010), the CCSS "are clearer and more rigorous than today's ELA standards in 37 states and today's math standards in 39 states."

The CCSS provide three key benefits:

◆ By setting forth a clear and consistent set of expectations for each grade level, the standards provide teachers and parents with what students should know and be able to do at every grade level, K–12. With common outcomes in place, next steps, including the design of curriculum and assessments, can benefit from the collaborative efforts of educators across the country. Additionally, parents and students will know the learning expectations, even if they move to a new school or state.

◆ The Common Core State Standards Initiative (www .corestandards.org) was able to develop learning standards informed by the most rigorous and successful models from states across the country as well as from countries around the world.

◆ These raised standards are aligned with college and twenty-first-century work expectations. The intent is to ensure that U.S. students will possess competencies that make them successful in the global marketplace.

The CCSS set rigorous benchmarks; however, their impact on student learning depends upon their implementation. True rigor encompasses high expectations for student learning, increased support so students can learn at higher levels, and the ultimate result of rigor—increased learning demonstrated by each student.

We cannot assume that simply adopting the standards provides a rigorous environment for students. Rigor is more than what you teach, it's how you teach and how students show you they understand. The CCSS are an excellent foundation for increasing rigor in your classroom; however, there are other integral aspects of rigor to consider.

High Expectations

Although we will discuss high expectations in depth in Chapter 6: Raise Expectations, let's look at them in the context of the CCSS. When we have high expectations for students, we begin with the standards. But then we must consider whether we truly believe students can meet the expectations identified in the new CCSS. For example, the language we use when teaching the standards can reflect high expectations or low ones.

High Expectation Language	Low Expectation Language
"The new standards may seem different, but you can do this."	"I know the new standards are hard, but the state says we have to do them anyway."
"You already know this. You'll just be applying what you know in a new way."	"I know you don't understand _____. It is because of these new standards."
"The standards may seem harder because they are new, but with my help you will be successful."	"Of course you don't understand _____. The new standards assume you learned something last year that you did not learn."

Next, the CCSS are geared toward the application of knowledge through higher-order thinking skills. Therefore, it will be natural to ask higher-order questions. The question remains, what do we do after we ask a question? How do we respond to students' answers? Do we press for more details or ask how and why follow-up questions? Do we probe partial information to help guide students to a deeper understanding? The cycle of questions, responses, questions, and more responses is a spiral to lead to higher learning.

Support

A second critical aspect of rigor is the increased support for student learning. There are a variety of ways to support students during the transition to new learning. First, make expectations clear to your students. Frequently, students don't learn because they did not understand the goal. Teachers can reframe the standards as questions for students to answer. Questions shift the perspective to the learner, as opposed to the teacher, and they tap into the investigative nature of learning. For a student, the question becomes, "What do I need to figure out?" versus "What is the teacher talking about today?"

Second, understand that scaffolding strategies will continue to be an integral part of your instruction. The exact strategy and tools you will need for your students depends on your individual situation (and on the individual learners), but they are still needed. If anything, the higher standards will demand an increased focus on using chunking, graphic organizers, metacognitive strategies, and many other tools to help students be successful. We'll look at multiple ways to support students in Chapter 4: Give Appropriate Support and Guidance.

Demonstration of Learning

The CCSS are to be accompanied by matching high-level assessments. It is likely that some of these assessments will be more useful to teachers than others, and the immediate emphasis appears to be on summative assessments. It is important that we not forget the critical role of formative assessments. As we ask students to move to a new set of standards that are much more challenging, they will likely struggle. One of the best scaffolding strategies we can use is to assess their work frequently in a manner that provides feedback so they can adjust what they are doing.

Second, it is imperative that we not allow students to fall through the cracks in this process. Formative assessments can provide information about each individual student so we can catch students at the point they need assistance. Keep in mind that formative assessments may be written or more formal, but the key is to assess each individual student.

Ultimately, the new CCSS are an excellent way to create immediate, rigorous expectations for students. However, standards, benchmarks, curriculum maps, and lesson plans are all just plans for the future or outlines of practice. They come to life in classrooms—places where risk taking is encouraged and supported, minds are challenged, and learning and learners are valued. Teachers carefully craft this environment.

Selecting Appropriate Texts

One of the major areas for increasing the difficulty level of content is through the texts used during teaching. Often, we use books or other materials that are not challenging for students. It seems there are two extremes: some students read only books that are too easy for them; others struggle with texts that are too difficult. It's important for students to read a book or an article they can quickly and easily finish; those opportunities build self-confidence, provide enjoyable experiences, and may increase student motivation. But if that's all students read, they never learn how to deal with more challenging materials.

Particularly at the upper grades, where we focus on reading to learn, we must help our students become independent learners who can capably handle our complex and changing world. A critical part of that process is teaching students to read and understand increasingly complex materials.

To increase rigor related to text selection, it is valuable first to simply assess whether students are reading texts that challenge them. Look for a balance: material should be difficult enough that students are learning something new, but not so hard that they give up. If you like to play tennis, you'll improve if you play against someone who is better than you. But if you play against Venus and Serena Williams, you'll learn less because you are overwhelmed by their advanced skill level. A good guideline is that for text to be appropriately challenging for growth, students should be able to understand about 75 percent of what they read. That percentage means students understand the majority of the material, while learning something new. One option for increasing text difficulty is to identify where your students are reading and provide text materials that match their level of growth.

As we look at how to incorporate this in a classroom, let me offer a caution. Text difficulty should never be a limiting factor for students. I visited one school where students were never allowed to choose something to read unless it was "within their point range." That is not what I am recommending. Students always need the opportunity to read texts of their choice. And there are some books that may have a lower score on a readability scale, but the content is more difficult, perhaps due to the concepts described or the use of figurative language.

However, I am saying that students need selected opportunities to read material that is appropriately rigorous. Please note the word *material*. Particularly with students who are reading substantially above or below their age or grade level, consider informational, nonfiction articles rather than novels or short stories. The use of informational material also supports the CCSS. Graphic novels and technology-based materials are another useful option. These help address issues other than just text difficulty. Remember, I am talking about depth, not length; students shouldn't feel as if they are being punished.

When I was teaching, I used books that were labeled on grade level, but in reality, they were much easier than what students were expected to read on the state test or in real-life materials. That is still true today, and that is why it is important to use a measure that is consistent across all texts, including standardized tests. No matter which tool you use to determine the difficulty of text materials, remember that text difficulty is only one factor to consider when selecting text for or with your students. Other considerations include the appropriateness of the text for the students' age or developmental levels, the content of the material, and the purpose for reading, such as for interest or research.

⇒ *Considerations for Text Selection*

Is the content of the text pertinent to my standards or
    objectives?
Is the content of the text appropriate to the purpose of the
    assignment (independent reading, research, partner
    reading, etc.)?
Is the content of the text appropriate to the age or develop-
    mental level of my students?
Is the content of the text appropriately challenging for
    growth (not too hard, yet not too easy)?
Is this the only opportunity my students will be given to read,
    or are they allowed choices at other times?

Lexile Framework

One tool for selecting text materials is the Lexile Framework, which defines a reader's ability in relation to the difficulty of text. It allows teachers and parents to understand a
reader's performance, whether on a standardized test or an
informal assessment, through examples of text materials, such
as books, newspapers, or magazines, that the reader can understand, rather than through a number such as a percentile. Since
the formula is based on sentence length and word frequency,
your professional judgment should factor into final decisions
about text. Benefits of the Lexile Framework include its inclu-
sion in the CCSS and the ability to level books along a "reading
thermometer" in a way that is proportional to the standardized
test used. You can find additional information about the Lexile
Framework and a searchable database of Lexile-leveled books
at www.lexile.com.

Notice I said to use "your professional judgment." Any
readability formula should be the starting point for book selection, but it should never be the only factor considered. The goal
is always to pick the right resource for the right reader at the

right time. Remember to think about all aspects of the book or text (see considerations on page 21) and preview materials to ensure they are appropriate for your students.

Goldilocks' Rules

Another option you may find more student-friendly is Goldilocks' Rules, which include the Five Finger Test. Lori Carter, author of the Book Nuts Reading Club Web site (www .booknutsreadingclub.com), uses the parallel to Goldilocks to provide questions your students can ask themselves to determine if a book is too easy, too hard, or just right!

Too Easy Books	1. Have you read this book many times before? 2. Do you understand the story very well without much effort? 3. Do you know and understand almost every word? 4. Can you read the book smoothly and fluently without much practice or effort?
Just Right Books	1. Is this book new to you? 2. Do you understand most of the book? 3. Are there a few words per page that you don't recognize or know the meaning of instantly? Remember to use the Five Finger Test. 4. Can someone help you with the book if you hit a tough spot?
Too Hard Books	1. Are there more than a few words on a page that you don't recognize or know the meaning of? Remember the Five Finger Test. 2. Are you confused about what is happening in most of the book? 3. When you read, are you struggling and does it sound choppy? 4. Is everyone busy and unable to help you if you hit a tough spot?

Source: www.booknutsreadingclub.com/goldilocksrule.html

Five Finger Test

1. First choose the book you think you would like to read.
2. Find a page of text somewhere in the middle of the book. Find a page with lots of text (words) and few or no pictures.

3. Begin to read the page. It is best to read the page aloud or in a whisper if possible while doing the test, so you can hear the places where you have difficulty.
4. Each time you come to a word you don't know, hold up one finger.
5. If you have all five fingers up before you get to the end of the page, wave the book good-bye. It is probably too difficult for you right now. Try it again later in the year. If you need help finding a book, ask your teacher or librarian.

Multiple Sources of Information

Another strategy to raise the level of content is to use multiple sources of information during your teaching or for assessments. Providing multiple sources can help students see a variety of perspectives, help students adjust to texts at varying levels of difficulty, and add depth to your instruction.

Varying Levels of Difficulty

One challenge in today's classrooms is the range of performance levels from students. When trying to pick one text to use, you have likely encountered this: it is too hard for some students, too easy for others, and an excellent choice for a few. Instead, I can differentiate by using multiple texts. For a lesson on rain forests, I might use the textbook section with the entire class. Next, students read a variety of articles on rain forests based on their reading levels. You can do this individually, but it's also appropriate to group students based on their reading levels. Students then "teach" their articles to the rest of the class. The resulting whole-group discussion of rain forests will be richer based on the expanded lesson.

Tim Conner, a teacher in Clayton County, Georgia, provides a different alternative. He groups his students, gives each group a different color marker, and asks them to write everything they know about the topic. As they rotate through a series of stations, the groups are given two minutes to add to the points written.

This is an excellent way for all students to participate and "teach" from their book or text without stand-up presentations.

Adding Perspective

A valuable skill for all subject areas and grade levels is to help students see differing perspectives through a variety of sources. As a social studies teacher explained, "Comparing secondary source information to primary source material helps students see what the writer or speaker intended rather than how other writers interpreted him or her." There are many options for written, audio, and video speeches available on the Internet, such as Martin Luther King Jr.'s "I Have a Dream," George W. Bush's speech just after the events of 9/11, or Susan B. Anthony's speech on a woman's right to vote. It's important to find a speech that suits your subject and the developmental age of your students. Career and technology teachers may wish to use speeches by leaders in specific professions, such as Steve Jobs or Suze Orman. Or if you've just read *The Very Hungry Caterpillar*, use an author interview with Eric Carle about his writing process, and discuss what students learned.

Other options include comparing opinion-based articles with news articles; texts written from different perspectives, such as the "Three Little Pigs" and "The True Story of the Three Little Pigs"; or examples of debates.

Adding Depth

In addition to adding perspective, the use of multiple texts allows students to look beyond the surface for more depth of information. For example, after reading the fictional book *The Watsons Go to Birmingham—1963*, by Christopher Paul Curtis, students can read nonfiction online, encyclopedia articles, and/or magazine articles to compare the story to Birmingham, Alabama, during the civil rights period. You could add another step by reading current newspaper and magazine articles to compare it to Birmingham today, detailing the changes that have occurred.

After reading the classic novel *The Sea Wolf*, by Jack London, students can read articles about schooners and the sealing industry. Instead of simply reading and discussing the story, students are required to use research skills, cite sources, and compare and contrast information from a variety of sources. The new activity requires all students to think at higher levels.

I often used newspapers in my classrooms. Students would read something that was clearly an opinion (such as an editorial or a letter to the editor) and assume it was factual. Comparing news stories to opinion pieces requires students to analyze and apply information. Similarly, reading a car insurance policy and the state driving laws allows students to see connections between cause (breaking a certain law) and effect (increased insurance rates).

⇒ Suggestions for Multiple Sources of Information

- Books by a particular author to compare style
- Job applications from different companies
- Videos on a news story (local versus national news; station considered "slanted" versus "balanced" station)
- YouTube videos on skateboarding to determine math skills involved

Finally, remember that text difficulty is only one factor to consider when selecting text for or with your students. Again, other considerations include the appropriateness of the text for students' age or developmental levels, the content of the material, and the purpose for reading, such as for interest or for research.

Depth, Not Coverage

In our culture, we are often bombarded with the message that more is better. We can find ourselves so focused on finishing the material before the end of the year that we only skim the surface. As a result, our students often log information in their short-term memory rather than truly learning and applying it in the future.

When it comes to rigor, less is more. If we expect students to learn at a high level, we must focus on depth of understanding, not breadth of coverage.

The major tool I used to help me focus on depth was a year-long planning guide. I mapped out all the units or topics for the year, added the standards, then listed lessons for each. Next, I laid out the entire pacing guide like a storyboard and used sticky notes to identify my estimated time for the unit. When I matched my estimates of time with the school calendar, I could see if I would be able to finish by the end of the year or if I had some extra days I could scatter throughout the year for "catch-up purposes."

I often hear teachers say, "I don't want to do that; it's just too overwhelming. I'll just plan a week at a time." But when we don't look at the overall picture, it's too easy to run out of time. Other teachers explain, "We've been handed a guide that dictates what we do every day." My best suggestion in that situation is to work within the parameters you are given, but it's still important to pay attention to where you need to spend extra time without sacrificing the entire schedule.

Beginning music teacher Tonya Woodell points out that depth for rigor is applicable to all subjects.

> The music standards would allow my students to play all grade-one pieces. The grading scale of music is set from one through six. Grade-six music is generally played by very good high school bands and colleges. Although I could allow my students to play only grade-one music, I expect them to be able to play grade-two and grade-three pieces. And they are able to do it! In choir, I could allow them to simply sing "crowd pleasing" songs. However, I expect my students to sing at least one foreign language piece a semester. I also expect that they sing in three-part harmony when unison or two-part would be acceptable.

One of today's challenges is the number and range of standards you are expected to teach. Larry Ainsworth recommends that you focus on "Power Standards," which are the standards and indicators essential for student success. He suggests focusing on standards that incorporate three elements:

> Endurance—Will this standard or indicator provide students knowledge and skills that will endure throughout a student's academic career and professional life?
>
> Leverage—Will this standard provide knowledge and skills that will be of value in multiple disciplines?
>
> Readiness for the next level of learning—Will this standard provide students with essential knowledge and skills that are necessary for success in the next grade level? (Ainsworth, 2003, p. 13)

He also provides a secondary set of criteria, which looks at the standards from the students' point of view. These three can be used interchangeably with the first set:

- ◆ School—what students need to know and be able to do at each level of learning.
- ◆ Life—what students will need to know and be able to do to be successful after formal schooling.
- ◆ Tests—concepts and skills most heavily represented on external high-stakes assessments (Ainsworth, 2011, p. 54).

This does not mean you ignore particular standards. Rather, you spend the most time on those that are the most critical.

With the adoption by many states of the new CCSS, a logical question is, "They are supposed to be streamlined; do I really need to prioritize?" In his new book, *Rigorous Curriculum Design*, Ainsworth responds to this question.

> As I prepared to read through the final version [of my book] . . . one question naturally came to mind: if there

are indeed fewer standards, will prioritization of the common standards even be necessary? I was naturally hopeful that the answer might be no—for the sake of educators and students—and then I found out that adopting states can also add up to fifteen percent of their existing state standards to the Common Core State Standards." (Ainsworth, 2011, p. 49)

Ainsworth also compiled a chart of the number of standards at each grade level, which shows the need to continue to prioritize. However, because of the streamlining of the standards, particularly in the area of vertical alignment, the job of prioritization should be simpler.

Conclusion

Raising the level of content for your students is one key way to increase rigor in your classroom. However, this doesn't mean simply choosing more difficult materials or increasing the amount of work students do. Rather, integrating strategies that allow you to help students move to more difficult content with your support will lead students to a deeper understanding of content.

⌁ Points to Ponder

Use the following sentence starters to reflect on the chapter.

I learned . . .

I'd like to try . . .

I need . . .

I'd like to share something from this chapter with . . .

3

Increase Complexity

The second broad strategy to increase rigor is to increase the complexity of your classroom instruction, both with existing activities and new ones.

Increase Complexity

Digging Deeper
Quality Questions
Ratchet Up Reviews
Take It Up a Notch

Digging Deeper

To encourage students to dig deeper than surface information, I used several questioning prompts and asked students to create their own questions about a text.

⇨ *Questioning Prompts*

What if . . .
How would it be different if . . .
Why couldn't . . .
If . . . then . . .

Jamie Kistler encouraged students to create their own questions as they read a short story. They wrote their questions on craft sticks, then played a game. If you prefer, you can give each student sticks of different colors so you know who created which question. You may also want to post a chart of question prompts, which is adapted from Kagan's Questioning Grid. Students drew a craft stick and had to answer the question. Because they had created the questions, they had more ownership in the game and were more engaged.

⇒ Questioning Prompts (Adapted from Kagan)

Who	Is
What	Did
When	Can
Where	Would
Why	Will
Which	Might

Chad Maguire, a teacher in the Charlotte-Mecklenburg Schools, chose an innovative way to push students to move beyond basic information. He assigned each of his students to research a famous mathematician. Then he gave bonus points for each item students found they had in common with the person they were researching. You might choose to incorporate that aspect into your regular grading rather than offering extra credit. Students were highly motivated to think about themselves and to move beyond the standard "This is when he/she was born. This is when he/she died. These are a few events that happened during his/her life."

In *Yellow Brick Roads*, Janet Allen (2000) describes an activity called "Flesh It Out." Give students a picture of a skeleton, and ask them to write different details about a character in a story or a person they are researching, such as their thoughts (brain), their actions (feet), or their words (mouth).

Flesh It Out

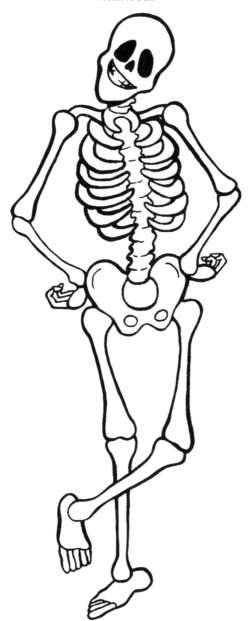

Skeleton drawing © 2008 Mike Sudduth & Carlee Lingerfelt. Used with permission.

It's also great as a wrap-up activity after students interview someone or hear a guest speaker. It helps students organize their thoughts, and it encourages them to move beyond standard information. I've worked with teachers to develop two options for the organizing points.

⇨ **Options for "Flesh It Out"**

Body Part	Adaptation One (characters or fiction)	Adaptation Two (research, current events, speaker)
Brain/Head	Thoughts	Ideas/Inventions
Mouth	Comment or something they would say	Quote or most important comment
Arms/Hands	Who they are connected to	What they created or did with their hands; network connections
Legs	Setting/places they visited, activities	Steps they took to be successful
Achilles tendon	Weaknesses or mistakes	Lessons learned/failures that led to success
Feet	Most important thing about character	Foundation of their life, key principle they discovered/lived by

A teacher shared on Twitter another great way to help students show a deeper understanding of a person. She uses the site www.myfakewall.com to have students create a fake Facebook wall about a character or person. Imagine the information students have to find to create a friends list, sample postings, family members, etc. This activity is also very motivating to our tech-savvy students. No matter what strategy you choose, helping students understand means giving them opportunities to show you what they know. And the more creative you are with your activities, the more engaged they are in learning.

Quality Questions

One of my favorite quotes is by Alice Wellington Rollins. She says, "The test of a good teacher is not how many questions he can ask his pupils that they will answer readily, but how many questions he inspires them to ask him which he finds it hard to answer."

Asking and answering questions is an everyday occurrence in most classrooms. Sometimes it happens orally, sometimes in writing, but it is one of the most common classroom activities. Good questioning helps students build understanding, but poor questioning can deter students from learning.

Levels of Questioning

There are many models for organizing higher levels of questions, but we will look at three. Each takes a slightly different approach and can be adapted for your precise purposes.

⇨ Models for Levels of Questioning

New Bloom's Taxonomy
Costa's House of Questions
Quality QUESTIONS

New Bloom's Taxonomy

The original Bloom's *Taxonomy of Educational Objectives*, released in 1956, was designed to help teachers write objectives and create tests to address a variety of levels of understanding. In 2001, a group of researchers revised the original taxonomy.

By crossing the knowledge row with the process column, you can plan objectives, activities, and assessments that allow students to learn different types of knowledge using a variety of processes. The widely used revised taxonomy is a complex but useful method for addressing all levels of questioning.

⇨ **Bloom's Taxonomy of Educational Objectives**

The Knowledge Dimension	The Cognitive Process Dimension					
	Remember	*Understand*	*Apply*	*Analyze*	*Evaluate*	*Create*
Factual	recognize	interpret	execute	organize	critique	construct
Conceptual	recall	classify	employ	disseminate	assess	produce
Procedural	define	summarize	implement	investigate	review	conceptualize
Metacognitive	distinguish	infer	perform	differentiate	judge	generate

Source: Anderson/Krathwohl/Airasian/Cruikshank/Mayer/Pintrich/Raths/Wittrock, *A Taxonomy for Learning, Teaching, and Assessing: A Revision of Bloom's Taxonomy of Educational Objectives* Abridged Edition, 1st © 2001. Printed and electronically reproduced by permission of Pearson Education, Inc., Upper Saddle River, New Jersey. Adapted by permission of the publisher.

Note: The verbs are interchangeable among the columns. For example, one could *recognize* factual, conceptual, procedural, and/or metacognitive information.

Costa's House of Questions

Costa and Kallick (2008), authors of *Learning and Leading With Habits of Mind*, provide a different model. It is a three-level, user-friendly, practical organizational tool for questioning.

Level One	Level Two	Level Three
Defining, identifying, naming, reciting, describing, listing, observing, scanning	Analyzing, contrasting, inferring, comparing, grouping, sequencing, synthesizing	Applying a principle, hypothesizing, judging, evaluating, imagining, predicting, speculating

Costa uses the metaphor of a three-story house to describe the levels of questioning. I've observed this model used in several AVID (Advancement Via Individual Determination, www.avid .org) classrooms, and it is effective for both students and teachers.

Quality QUESTIONS

Finally, no matter which model of questioning you use, it's important to reflect on the quality of questions you create. Here are nine reminders, around the acrostic of QUESTIONS, to help guide your development of questions during lessons.

⇒ *Characteristics of Good Questioning*

Q—quality
Don't waste your time on questions that are unclear, confusing, or irrelevant.
U—understanding
Make sure your questions lead to an understanding of content.
E—encourage multiple responses
Questions with more than one answer lead to higher levels of thinking.

S—spark new questions
  *If your question encourages students to ask more questions,
  you've struck gold!*
T—thought-provoking
  *Prompting students to think is the truest aim of good
  questions.*
I—individualized
  Customize questions to your content and to your students.
O—ownership shifted to students
  Give students the opportunity to create their own questions.
N—narrow and broad
  *Some questions are focused, some more open-ended. Use a
  balance.*
S—success building
  *Remember the goal of all questioning: successful student
  learning.*

As you create and/or adapt lessons to incorporate more rigorous opportunities for learning, you may want to consider the questions that are embedded within your instruction. I recently talked with a teacher who was using higher standards and more complex activities, but she asked her students basic recall or memory-based questions to assess their understanding. That defeats the purpose. Higher-level questioning, which includes probing or extending questions, is an integral part of a rigorous classroom.

Success Building

Ultimately, all these recommendations lead to the critical purpose of good questioning—helping your students build to successful learning. Questions are not simply part of your lesson; they are the key to unlocking understanding for students. Too often, we ask students to read or listen to something, and then we assume they know it. Real understanding is more than that, and it doesn't happen through osmosis. It happens when students interact with knowledge in a way that enables them to connect it to what they already know and to their own experiences. Good questioning helps them with the process and ensures their success.

As you create questions for your students, remember to build in questions that are open-ended, that have more than one answer. Although it is important to ask questions about facts and details that have only one answer, higher-level questions generally have several possible responses. The how and why questions will prepare students for life after school. Another way to promote analytical thinking is to follow up on students' responses. Even if a question has a one-word answer, ask your students "How do you know?" "Why did you decide on that answer?" or "What information led you to think that?" By integrating these types of extending questions, you are teaching your students to reflect on their own thinking.

Ratchet Up Reviews

On one of my school evaluation visits, a young boy stopped me in the hall. After I explained my purpose in the school, I asked if he liked school. He replied, "It's pretty easy here. We already know the stuff they teach." His point, that we often spend too much time reviewing basic content with our students, has merit. I am not suggesting that you stop reviewing content that your students don't understand. However, if students don't know what a fraction is by the time they are in high school, completing pages of practice problems likely won't help.

I struggled with that, too. I had students who simply did not understand basic concepts; teaching them more-advanced content seemed impossible. But I learned a key lesson: repeating the same information again, only slower or louder, doesn't work. A more effective strategy is shifting to a more difficult, authentic purpose for using basic knowledge and then answering questions to help students complete the assignment.

When it was evident that my students did not fully understand how to compare and contrast information, I created a folder game. Each group of students was given a folder with a picture from a newspaper or magazine article pasted on the front. The actual article was glued on the inside. Students were directed to look at the picture without opening the folder. Then, individually, each student wrote as many words as possible about the picture, one word per sticky note. Since they were writing only words, the one-inch by one-inch size of a sticky note was adequate. Next, the students in the group talked to one another and used all their words to create a sentence about the picture. Usually, someone asked to add words, such as *the* or *and*, or to add punctuation. That gave me a quick teachable moment to discuss grammar and sentence structure. Then I told them they could write anything they needed on more notes.

If you want to stop at this point, students can individually write a descriptive paragraph about the picture. For students who don't know how to begin, they have a group sentence as a starting point. Each group also has a customized word bank of leftover words to use in the paragraph.

This activity can be used across a variety of content areas as we move to the next step. Students opened the folder and read the accompanying article, which was chosen to match a specific topic and standards. By comparing their sentences with the actual article, students must use analytical skills. Students used an assessment scale (see "Scale for Comparing Sentences and Articles") to determine how their work measured up, and they could revise their sentence if needed.

⇨ Scale for Comparing Sentences and Articles

1. The sentence is completely reflective of the article and could be included in the story seamlessly.
2. Parts of our sentence would fit into the article.
3. Were we looking at the same picture?

Sharing their responses incorporated elements of comparison and contrast and typically led to a rich discussion of how a picture does not always tell the full story. This allowed me to teach strategic reading and thinking through application, rather than simply telling them they needed to be strategic readers. It's important to choose articles linked to what you are teaching or reviewing in order to help students see the connection of reading with learning your content.

Robyn Galloway, a teacher in Kentucky, shared a very effective instructional strategy for review. She explains:

> It's called affinity. Students acquire information through reading, presentations, or multimedia. Then they write everything they learned on sticky notes (three-inch by three-inch or three-inch by five-inch size). Each fact, event, person, etc., is written on a note—one piece of information per note. Next, students form groups of four or five participants. Together, they group their information, looking for patterns and differences.

This is excellent, as students can pursue further research to determine if isolated facts (those that only one student noted) are true. It's also a perfect way to have students compare different videos, texts, or other sources.

Missy Miles uses a game called "Will the Real Christopher Columbus Please Stand Up" with her social studies students. She explains,

> The students stand at their desks, and I go around the room asking them questions about Christopher Columbus or another historical figure we have been studying. If a student gets the question wrong, he or she must sit down. The level of questions increases in complexity as the game goes on, until there's only one "Christopher Columbus" left standing. The students love reviewing this way. Later in the year, we ask them to create and bring in the questions and answers for the review. Each student writes three to four questions of various levels and puts them in the bank of questions I pull from for the game!

Take It Up a Notch

Finally, in addition to trying new strategies, you can simply take existing strategies "up a notch." For example, a middle school teacher was concerned he would be required to write new tests, because each test had a few true-false questions included. I explained that if he wanted to keep those questions, he could add more rigor by requiring students to correct any false answers. Instead of guessing, students would then have to demonstrate they understood what was not correct about the statement.

While working with teachers in Pasadena, Texas, I was contacted by a group of primary teachers who was concerned. In the math homework the teachers used, there was a final question that asked students to explain their thinking about a particular problem. However, due to the number of at-risk students and second language learners, the students could not even read the question, so the teachers had no way of knowing if they could explain their thinking. The solution? Ask the question verbally, so that students begin to understand it, then use the question, perhaps with a rewording so that reading is not a stumbling block to rigor, and then move to the standard question.

I recently received the following assignment used in a tenth-grade honors course. Students had a week to complete the project. I've reproduced the assignment sheet, as typed, including bold and capitalization.

History Project #1 _____   Due: (one week) _____

Wanted Poster

We have studied several individuals who made significant contributions during the Renaissance and Reformation. You will create a wanted poster about one of these people. The information on the poster must include:

1. Poster **MUST** be on an 8½ × 11 sheet of paper.   **(10 points)**
2. Mug shot—We need to know what they look like!   **(10 points)**
3. First and Last name of your historical figure.   **(5 points)**
4. Birth Date and Year of Death.   **(5 points)**
5. What country were they born in **and** where did they do their work?   **(10 points)**
6. What are they famous (wanted) for? 5–8 complete sentences, in your own words, for full credit.   **(30 points)**
7. A fact that you found interesting **OR** a quote by the person.   **(10 points)**
8. Print out or photocopy of your sources with info highlighted.   **(15 points)**
9. Your name on the bottom right corner.   **(5 points)**

There were 45 names on the sheet. The teacher cut the names apart and had the students draw a name and told them they were leaving it to "fate" to decide whom they would profile. When asked if they could switch names, they were told, "Absolutely not!"

There are several ways to increase the rigor of this assignment. Currently, students earn credit simply for completing the assignment. Scoring should be based on quality rather than quantity. I would revise the point breakdown for the Wanted Poster. Students would also need to see models, along with a rubric detailing the expectations for an A, a B, a C, a D, or an F. Keep in mind that earning an A or a B demonstrates exceeding expectations, not simply meeting them.

⇨ *Revision of Grading for Wanted Poster*

Percentage of Grade	Requirements
20%	Connections: narrative includes key life events, family, possible associates, other locations visited or other places the person lived to help with locating person.
25%	Synthesis based on multiple sources (minimum of 5): information in paper is synthesized and confirmed from multiple sources, rather than summarized from an isolated source. It is also cited appropriately to demonstrate synthesis.
25%	Analysis: as a conclusion, narrative includes an analysis of the individual, including strengths, weaknesses, and possible other contributions the person could have made to the movement. Although your opinion, analysis should be based on the information gathered.
20%	Written narrative: overall flow and quality of writing, appropriate information included, extraneous information excluded. Quotes and other information support key points made throughout the paper.
10%	Basic requirements: completion of all aspects of assignment, 8" × 10" paper, "mug shot," your name at bottom right corner, reference list in appropriate format on reference page, word-processed narrative with 12-point font and 1-inch margins, minimum of 5 sources, and photocopy of sources with information highlighted.

You may also want to use the "Flesh It Out" graphic organizer or other prewriting activities to help students organize their information and move deeper into their research.

Conclusion

Increasing the complexity of your instruction does not mean starting over. There are a variety of ways you can increase the complexity of your existing activities and assessments, as well as integrating new ones, throughout the year.

⚙ Points to Ponder

Use the following sentence starters to reflect on the chapter.

I learned . . .

I'd like to try . . .

I need . . .

I'd like to share something from this chapter with . . .

4

Give Appropriate Support and Guidance

The third strategy to increasing rigor is to increase the amount of support and guidance throughout your instruction to help students be successful. There are many ways to support students, so keep in mind this is an introduction to scaffolding, focusing on four areas.

Give Appropriate Support and Guidance

Modeling
Gradual Release
Working With Struggling Learners
Extra Help and Support

Modeling

Modeling strategies are critical for helping your students succeed. If we give only a set of directions, students can become confused.

Thinking Aloud

Think-alouds are a critical part of every teacher's repertoire. When you "think aloud," you're simply verbally explaining what you are thinking. Many students simply have no idea of the processes used when learning new information. They see learning as the code that is unbreakable because they don't have the key. What we know as teachers is that there are multiple steps that go into any learning process, and one way to break that down for our students is by modeling our thinking.

Here's a sample of a think-aloud for students.

I'm not sure I understood this word. But the author is writing about earth's atmosphere, and the sentence right after uses the word *pollution*, so I'm paying attention to how the environment is affected by exhaust fumes or other chemicals.

Or,

When I first read this, I thought that the point was the value of democracy. But then I realized that the text is comparing different types of government because there was a summary of each type of government without a perspective of the best one.

See how simple it is? In fact, it's so basic, we assume everyone else knows how to talk through that process. Your strong students do that in their heads, but your struggling students do not understand it. That's why it's important to model your thinking for students.

For my son, this is especially important in his math class. He can "get all jumbled up in the word problems," and he is more successful when his teacher walks students through her thinking process. You can follow the same process with any instruction. The purpose is to show your students how you are processing information.

Many of your students simply need to understand what is in your head. As one teacher told me, "Most students turn in their best idea of what we are looking for. Sometimes they really don't know what we are thinking, and it's our job to make sure they do know." That defines this strategy: support, engage, and motivate your students to higher levels of learning by making sure they actually understand what they are expected to do.

Model and Mimic

Kendra Alston is more formal in her modeling instruction. She holds "Watch What I Do" days. On one of those days, she picks a specific skill and models it throughout the lesson. Her students take notes on what she does, completing the left-hand column of a chart. Then they complete the right-hand column, thinking about how they can do the same thing. The next day is "You Do It Too," when students apply what they learned by doing it themselves.

⇒ Watch What I Do... Then You Do It Too!

What Did I Do?	What Will You Do?

Technology for Modeling

Jessica Chastain uses technology to clarify her expectations for students' participation in their first student-led portfolio assessment conferences. As she explains,

> I taped a sample interview to give the students a good idea of what to expect. When the class viewed the sample interview, I would stop the video after each question, have the students repeat each question to me, and then they would write it down. The second time through, we watched the whole interview with no interruptions. Then we discussed it. When I interviewed the students throughout the next week, they were prepared to share their work with me, offer me their opinions of

their strengths and weaknesses, and we were able to set a goal for the next part of the year.

Since she knew this would be challenging for her students, Jessica showed them a virtual example of the entire process, as well as providing instruction to ensure their success. You can easily use other technology tools, such as online videos, to help students understand what they are expected to do.

Gradual Release

Helping students take ownership of their learning is important. One day you won't be there for them, and your students need to be independent. But you can't just give your students work and leave them alone. You need to structure opportunities that allow them to take ownership, and teach them how to grow. A good comparison for this approach is learning to ride a bike. I remember riding a tricycle when I was growing up. I was very good at it and felt quite confident of my abilities. At some point, I got a "real bike" for Christmas. My parents, in their wisdom, put training wheels on it while I learned to ride. Those extra wheels provided stability and balance as I learned how to ride it. Then Dad took the training wheels off. He taught me to ride without the training wheels, but he was beside me with one hand on the seat. One day, he let go of the seat, and I realized I was riding by myself. I was so excited. I had learned to ride a bike, and I loved it.

Instruction for Independence

The key to developing independent learners is to teach them how. As Jill Yates says,

I learned early on that I had to make no assumptions in believing that my students naturally knew what was expected, how to transition, and what being accountable and responsible for good choices meant. I have come to realize that my explicit consistency and modeling are what create and sustain the strong foundational and operational understanding I seek. And I have found this in turn creates classes that desire and choose to pursue success, confidence, and pride.

Be the Expert

Another way Kendra Alston helps her students become independent is to use the "Be the Expert" game. With a partner, students read a section of text. Next, each student assumes a role: one student is the expert, the other is the amateur. Kendra tells the amateur, "Pretend you don't know about the topic; what questions would you ask?" The amateur student asks questions, and the expert gives answers about the topic. Kendra picks the expert initially, but after each section of text, the students switch roles. Students also log questions and answers, which provides an informal assessment.

⇨ Expert/Amateur

| Amateur (question) |
| Expert (answer) |
| Amateur (question) |
| Expert (answer) |

This activity can be used with any grade level or subject area. For example, after reading informational articles about a topic in your content area, students can review the content as experts and amateurs.

Janelle Hicks builds a strong foundation for independence with her kindergarten students.

I do a lot during reading and writing workshop. I model for the students but then encourage them to "try it out." During writing, I will praise those students who try something new and invite them to share their writing with the rest of the class. As the children develop reading strategies and have the opportunity to practice them during independent reading, I find that this helps them to become independent readers and writers.

Other options that allow students to become more independent include signing contracts, working in groups, and carrying out individual projects. That's the way to help your students succeed. Show them how, then let them try!

Working With Struggling Learners

What about students who, for whatever reason, have fallen behind in learning and are struggling? For example, Durrell is a student with lots of potential; his fifth-grade teacher sees this and has identified several talents that are particularly strong. He is very creative, which comes out in his writing—on the rare occasions when he writes without worrying about what he is writing. His major issue is that he doesn't trust his own judgment/opinion.

What can you do as a teacher to help the "Durrells" in your class? Steve Siebold (stevesiebold.com), a mental toughness consultant, compares the thought processes of an amateur performer and a professional performer. They are remarkably applicable to students like Durrell. After all, what we ask students to do in learning is performance to them! We can adapt Steve's comparative categories to learning: amateurs are nonstrategic learners; professionals are strategic learners.

Nonstrategic (Amateur) Learners	Strategic (Professional) Learners
Doesn't think about thinking (no metacognition).	Thinks about thinking—a lot, even without realizing it (metacognition).
Perspective of Self and Others	
Places high value on the opinions of others (needs constant reassurance).	Is confident of own decisions.
Has external frame of reference.	Has internal locus of control.
Asks for help first without trying to work out problem on own.	Asks for help only after using toolkit of own strategies.
Connections	
Doesn't connect learning to other things unless made explicit by the teacher—doesn't realize that all connects to long term.	Thinks about the "what if . . ."; always makes connections in head to self, other learning experiences, and future/real life.
Cannot visualize an end product or a correct result of task or learning—doesn't know what it "feels like to be right."	Can visualize the end product or result of task or learning—is confident of correctness and/or being right.
Views About Failure	
Views failure as the end, not as a learning process.	Learns from failures/views failure as a learning process.
Uses feedback and criticism as a stop sign.	Uses feedback and criticism to improve.
Problems and Solutions	
Cannot conceive of plans for what to do if what they are told to do doesn't work.	Plans for the unexpected and deals with those things/has alternate plans.
Is overwhelmed by problems.	Deals with one problem at a time.

Using this information can help us understand our students' behaviors and reactions. It does not replace formal or formative assessments; however, it does help us adjust our support. Let's look at each of these beliefs and how they impact literacy learning.

⇨ Beliefs That Impact Learning

- ◆ Perspective of Self and Others
- ◆ Connections
- ◆ Views About Failure
- ◆ Problems and Solutions

Perspective of Self and Others

When working with students like Durrell, begin by recognizing the real issue. He isn't simply bugging you, he truly doesn't trust in or believe in himself or his judgment. There is no short-term solution to changing beliefs, but there are actions you can take to support students like Durrell. First, when he comes to you for help, don't just give the answer, which may only encourage the dependency. Instead, ask him what he thinks and keep asking until you get an answer. You may have to encourage; you may have to wait; you may have to ask multiple times; but keep at it until he starts thinking about what he's asking. Provide positive reinforcement when he attempts to figure it out independently first, even if he isn't right. Then provide more positive reinforcement for ultimately solving the problem himself.

You might also allow him to ask some other students for help, but that should be limited. I have used the rule "Ask Three Before Me," meaning a student should ask three students before asking me a question, but it's limited to three. That may sound a little complicated, but it's like any other routine—if you take time to teach it to students, you save time later. Just count how many times students come to you for very basic, simple questions (What page did you say? Which problems? Where did you say to put this paper?).

Look for opportunities to praise him for working out a solution on his own to reinforce that positive behavior. Also, help him develop a list of the strategies he can use to solve problems. If your student keeps a journal, have him designate a section and keep a log of strategies that have worked for him in the past. For example, if drawing a picture helps him remember a key concept, he should write that down so he will remember it next time.

You might also choose to teach him a structured way of dealing with some common issues, such as encountering new vocabulary words. Some of my students had one response for figuring out the new word: ask me! So I developed a simple set of procedures for what to do when they didn't know a new word. They quickly learned to try other options before they came to me.

Connections

On the other hand, nonstrategic learners don't even realize they are thinking, even when they are thinking negative thoughts. Durrell isn't connecting learning to himself or any other content unless you tell him. He feels like learning is a word search puzzle, with information hidden inside other letters, and he doesn't know where to look. To help him make connections, provide clear modeling of your thinking.

Amateur learners also don't seem to make the connection between what you ask them to do and what it would look like if he or she was successful. I had one student who turned in a book report, and in exasperation, I said, "Were you even in the room when I explained this?" The reality was that Brianna gave me what she thought I wanted, but she didn't understand. I've learned that the most important thing I can do to help my students with this issue is to show them multiple examples of what "good" looks like.

Views About Failure

A second difference between the strategic and the nonstrategic learner is how students view failure. Some students expect to be perfect on the first try (and don't we all want that!). But when that doesn't happen, there are two choices. For struggling students, anything short of "being right," which includes receiving feedback and/or constructive criticism, becomes a stop sign—a symbol of failure. For Durrell, the voice in his head says, "Because you missed it on the first try, you're a failure, so you might as well give up." This is compounded by the fact that Durrell had no plan for what to do if what he was told to do did not work. He tried to read the story and use pictures to help understand the story, but that didn't work, so he gave up. This contrasts with strategic learners, who use feedback and criticism to improve because they view failure as a learning process. They recognize that failure happens to everyone, and that success comes from building off failures.

With my students, I openly discussed the role of failure in success, giving personal examples as appropriate to show that everybody fails. I'll never forget the night I brought my graduate students an article I'd written that had been rejected by an educational journal. They assumed I'd never experienced rejection, and it was helpful for them to see me respond to that in a positive way. We all have times we are not successful—it's important to show students how to overcome those times. Also, encourage your students who do try, particularly if they are not successful on the first attempt.

Problems and Solutions

A related issue is that nonstrategic learners expect to do the same thing and get different results. So the last time he had to do a project, Durrell waited until the last minute, didn't have the resources to complete it, and made an F. For the next project, he did the same thing. He didn't see that working ahead of time and pulling together resources in advance would make a difference. Encouraging and reinforcing effort are particularly critical for those students who do not understand the importance of their own efforts. In *Classroom Instruction that Works*, Marzano, Pickering, and Pollock (2001) make two important comments regarding students' views about effort.

⇨ *Research-Based Generalizations About Effort*

◆ Not all students realize the importance of believing in effort.

◆ Students can learn to change their beliefs to an emphasis on effort.

(Marzano et al., 2001, p. 50)

Strategic learners also make plans for the unexpected. Playing "What If" allows them to deal with the unexpected. They also recognize that you must change what you do to get different results, which comes from a strong internal belief that they are responsible for results. To help your struggling students make the shift, plan with them. Before they begin a project, ask them to list several things they can do to be successful. Build the lists in small groups, and share the most important items with everyone. Then remind them throughout the project of the strategies, also giving them some suggestions of ways to deal with problems.

To counter students' feelings of being overwhelmed, chunk your projects or activities. This can be as simple as listing specific steps for completion on the board. You are really just helping them write a to-do list, but it makes a difference. For long-term projects, require students to turn in pieces in smaller "bites," and highlight for everyone the specific step they should be working on.

There is not a lockstep formula that works for each student, but realizing that students' actions are based on beliefs about who they are and how they learn will help you adapt your instruction to support them. And don't assume this is just for students who are working below grade level. I've seen these characteristics with some of my gifted students. They can struggle with a perfectionist approach to failure that keeps them from moving forward in learning.

Extra Help and Support

In an ideal world, we would teach a lesson, and each of our students would understand the content and use the information to achieve higher levels of learning. But that does not always happen. Some students immediately grasp the material and move forward, but others need additional assistance.

Providing appropriate extra help to students can be a challenge. First, there is the pressure to make sure everyone moves through the curriculum in time for the test. Then there are the times you teach and teach and teach and just don't understand why your students don't understand. But that's the exact moment they need you to keep going. If you are frustrated, imagine how they feel! There are seven key characteristics of effective support.

⇨ Effective Support

S—structured
U—understanding is the result
P—personalized
P—positive support
O—options within lesson and outside class
R—repetition-less
T—timeliness

Structured

First, effective support is structured. There is a plan to monitor student learning and provide extra help. Sometimes, students don't realize they need help. If you build in opportunities to assess student understanding at key points, you are better able to provide immediate help to students. You can do this formally with a test, but that may be too late. Create ways to assess your students' understanding within each lesson or at the end of your class so you can immediately address any issues.

I used partner activities to do this in my lessons. After I taught a particular concept, I asked students to turn to a partner and explain the concept. Then partners would share with another pair. Finally, I'd ask groups of four to write a short summary for the group, including any questions they might have. This made it safe for students to share information and to ask questions.

Another easy way to assess is with exit slips. As students are leaving your class, their ticket to get out of the door is to give you a piece of paper with three sentences.

Exit Slip

What I learned today.

How this connects to something else I know.

A question I still have.

Exit slips allow you to quickly see what your students learned and areas of confusion. And it is a great tool to give you information to plan your next lesson. You can ask students to do this anonymously, or they can put their names on the slips so you can work with individual students. Just be sure to have a plan. The structure will help you help them learn.

Understanding Is the Result

Effective support always results in a deeper understanding of the content rather than memorization of facts. As I learned, if a student does not understand decimals, more practice doesn't help. We need to find different ways to present the information so that students internalize what they are learning.

Christy Matkovich points out that teachers must find a way to deliver information to students "so their brains learn it. It might be by drawing a picture or through movement. If your form of delivery isn't working, then find a different way to deliver it." Ideally, your lesson includes enough options for each student to learn. But if some students don't, then it's up to you to find a new way to help them understand.

Sometimes the best help comes from another student rather than the teacher. As Shannon Knowles explains,

> I regularly have one student who understands and explains the concepts to those who don't. Sometimes, they explain to everyone in class, sometimes to the one or two who need it. They just say it in a way that makes more sense to the students.

Personalized

Good support is also personalized to each student's needs. In order to customize the support, you'll need to learn as much as possible about each student. To connect with your students, it's important to learn about their interests, learning styles, strengths, and weaknesses.

Positive Support

It's also critical to provide support in a positive manner. Recently, one of my new graduate students was struggling with a research paper. She was returning to school after an extended break, and finding research electronically was a new skill for her. After class, she made an appointment to meet with me individually for help. By the time she left my office, I thought everything was fine. One week later, she called me at home, quite upset. It seems she did understand what to do, but when she tried to find research on her own, she struggled. She hesitated to call me since I'd already shown her how to use the online resources twice (once in class, once individually). We met the next day, and after we worked together, she immediately went to the computer lab to try it again on her own, this time with success. She was grateful and commented that I didn't seem to mind helping her again. If I had frowned, grumbled, or commented that she just wasn't paying attention, she would not have been as successful. Positive, ongoing encouragement of your students is a critical part of your role as a teacher.

Options Within Lessons and Outside Class Time

Make effective support available during your lessons and outside class time. The most effective help comes during a lesson when confusion is fresh in your students' minds. You don't want them to go home and practice something incorrectly. That is where partner-sharing activities are helpful; they help assess and ensure understanding at multiple points during the lesson. But for those students who need extra one-on-one time, provide opportunities for them to meet with you after class. Another common experience occurs when a student understands the material in class, but twenty-four hours later, he or she is confused. It's important to have regular times you are available for those students willing to ask for help.

Repetition-less

In one of my workshops, a teacher said, "I know how to provide help for my students. Help means extra practice. The more help they need, the more homework I assign." That is not effective support. Repetition works only when memorizing isolated facts, and even that provides only short-term learning.

Repetition rarely provides long-term learning. As Christy Matkovich says,

> Practice needs to be quality. If the day didn't go well, if my students are lost or confused, then we'll just go home and start over the next day. If I send homework on a day like that, they'll create a way to do it, then we have to unlearn!

It's harder to "unteach" bad learning than it is to invest extra time in making sure your students truly understand. If I don't understand something, practicing it over and over again doesn't help. Hearing it again, told to me in the same words only slower or louder doesn't help. Find ways to reteach information through learning centers or other hands-on activities.

Timeliness

Finally, effective support is provided in a timely manner. If you wait two weeks after students ask for your help, you've lost your opportunity. Confusion is like a snowball rolling down a hill. It only gets larger. The longer you allow your students to be confused, the worse it gets. That's why you need to build in effective structures to ensure that students who need help are able to obtain it immediately, which prevents larger problems from occurring later.

Create positive ways to support your students in your classroom to ensure their understanding at every step of the learning process. The time you invest will pay off as you see the light of understanding in your students' eyes.

Despite your efforts during class, your students may need extra help outside your regular class time. For some students, they simply need more time and individual attention.

There are lots of great ideas for providing extra help and support to students, but it's best to find a method that works in your situation. Also, I'd encourage you to work with administrators and other teachers toward a school-wide plan. In this way, you can share the extra commitment.

Finally, it's important to remember that some of your students who need the most help rarely ask for it. You might consider looking at ways that require your most struggling students to receive extra help. Unfortunately, the students who are struggling the most don't even realize they need help. Others are embarrassed to ask for assistance. Finding ways to help all your students is challenging, but essential.

Conclusion

Giving appropriate support to students is a critical aspect of increasing rigor. Although we have looked at four strategies, I encourage you to read *Classroom Instruction that Works*, by Robert Marzano, Debra Pickering, and Jane Pollock (2001). It includes nine research-based strategies that are effective across grade levels and content areas.

⇨ *Research-Based Strategies for Effective Classroom Instruction*

1. Identifying similarities and differences
2. Summarizing and note taking
3. Reinforcing effort and providing recognition
4. Homework and practice
5. Nonlinguistic representations
6. Cooperative learning
7. Setting objectives and providing feedback
8. Generating and testing hypotheses
9. Cues, questions, and advance organizers

There are many other sources of information regarding support, including some that are specific to certain subjects or grade ranges. It is important to use the ones discussed in this chapter only as a starting point and build from there.

💡 Points to Ponder

Use the following sentence starters to reflect on the chapter.

I learned . . .

I'd like to try . . .

I need . . .

I'd like to share something from this chapter with . . .

5

Open Your Focus

The fourth strategy to increasing rigor in your classroom is to open the focus of your activities. This provides students opportunities to apply problem solving, creativity, and higher-order thinking skills to learning. You'll also note that we discuss some reading strategies in this chapter. For upper grade levels and specific content areas, these strategies are applicable to help your students understand your content more effectively. Additionally, they can support the new emphasis on reading across all content areas in the new Common Core State Standards.

> **Open Your Focus**
>
> *Begin With Discovery*
> *Choices*
> *Perspectives*
> *Connections*

Begin With Discovery

One of the most common forms of instruction is to start with information and then have students apply it in some type of real-life situation. Although that allows students to move to higher-order thinking through application, there is another alternative. Instead, what would happen if we opened our instruction, asking students to think and discover on their own?

I love the story of George Dantzig that Cynthia Kersey wrote about in *Unstoppable* (2005).

> As a college student, George studied very hard and always late into the night. So late that he overslept one morning, arriving 20 minutes late for class. He quickly copied the two math problems on the board, assuming they were the homework assignment. It took him several days to work through the two problems, but finally he had a breakthrough and dropped the homework on the professor's desk the next day.
>
> Later, on a Sunday morning, George was awakened at 6 a.m. by his excited professor. Since George had been late for class, he hadn't heard the professor announce that the two unsolvable equations on the board were mathematical mind teasers that even Albert Einstein hadn't been able to answer. But George, working without any thoughts of limitation, had solved not one, but two problems that had stumped mathematicians for thousands of years.

I sometimes wonder what my students would learn if I didn't package everything together for them. One day, instead of telling them the objective for the day, I decided to let them figure it out. I named multiple cities, such as Raleigh, Sacramento, and Albany. After a few seconds, one student shouted, "Hey, I know—those are all state capitals!" This is an easy way to begin your class focused on students' discovery of the topic, and it can be used at any grade level. A kindergarten teacher can use it to introduce the color of the day, pulling items out of a box. A science teacher can use this strategy to introduce elements or subatomic particles.

Stepping it up a notch, Lindsay Yearta uses the "Red Herring" game with her students. She gives multiple examples that are linked, but students must identify the red herring—the one that does NOT belong. As your students become more confident, they can take ownership and individually or in small groups create their own examples for the class. This is a great adaptation that adds another level of rigor.

Other Ways to Help Students Make Discoveries

Another common activity is to show students a picture and ask them what it is, or what they observe. To ratchet up the rigor, cut up the picture into puzzle pieces. First, ask the students to make a prediction from an individual piece. Then add a piece at a time, seeing what students can list as known facts from the single pieces. When the puzzle is finished, compare the complete picture with the "facts" they surmised. This can be done with a whole group using technology or a paper picture, or you can break students into small groups and give each a piece of the puzzle.

While I was at Lincoln Heights Elementary, one of the primary grade teachers adapted this idea. She put the entire picture in a file folder. She had cut two eyes and a smile out of the front of the folder, and asked her young students to "try to guess the picture just from the eyes and smile. They loved it!" Again, you can also use this idea with technology-based instructional tools.

Next, take your standards, whether they are the new Common Core State Standards or your state standards, and turn them into questions. What one question would you want students to be able to answer if they learned what they needed to from your lesson? In other words, if you move past the educational language and extra information, what is the one core thing your students should be able to know or do? What is your focus question? Starting with a question rather than a statement shifts the ownership to your students and immediately engages them.

You can also end your lessons or units with an application-oriented, open-ended project to prompt students' thinking. Darrin Baird, a career and technology teacher at Jellico High School, assigned his students to small groups. Then he gave each group a box of Cheerios and asked them to create something new with the cereal. Finally, each group developed a marketing plan for the invention. It was an excellent way to have students apply the marketing concepts they were learning in class.

⇨ Sample Open-Ended Projects

Design a robot that can play a particular sport.

As a producer of a music video, design your budget, using accurate costs for each portion of the production.

After reading "The Three Little Pigs," research the cost of building each house.

As a talk show host, write questions and answers used during your televised interview with Aztec Indians. (This works much more effectively if students act out and record the interview.)

You are the teacher. Create the perfect classroom.

Create the criteria for acceptable apps—you are a venture capitalist.

Using discovery as a tool for learning is not new; it's a very effective method for instruction. You can find multiple examples of projects, and more detailed instructional activities and strategies by searching for problem-based learning on the Internet. In a recent meta-analysis by Robert Marzano (2001), he notes that although discovery learning is more effective than direct instruction, guided discovery is the most effective. The keys are to provide scaffolding as students move through the process and to focus on your purpose—to help students learn at higher levels through a process of discovery.

Choices

Offering choices is one of the simplest ways to encourage student involvement in your classroom. Unfortunately, I talk to many students who feel as though they never have any choices. I spoke with one student who told me he felt like school was a place where "they tell you what to do all the time." Feeling a lack of choice is disheartening and frustrating for anyone.

There are many opportunities for students to have choices in your classroom. It's fairly easy to give students choices with a little extra planning. One of the most basic ways is to allow students to choose how they demonstrate understanding of content. They can create videos, write a series of blog entries, develop a talk show, write a journal from the perspective of a historical figure, create a game, or act in a dramatic scene. Often, their products are more advanced than that of a standard assignment.

Many teachers use individual learning contracts, which contain a list of activities related to the unit. Students complete a certain number of the tasks, depending on the grade they desire. However, be careful that your assessment includes a focus on quality and doesn't just consider completion of the projects. If you would like a more creative approach, you can turn those choices into a tic-tac-toe grid. By providing choices of rigorous activities, you can ensure all students demonstrate learning at a high level. You may also consider designing activities for your contracts or tic-tac-toe grids around the multiple intelligences. This helps you provide a wide variety of options for your students.

⇨ Sample Tic-Tac-Toe Activities

- Design a proposal for a venture capitalist for a game based on the content.
- Choose one character from the story/book. Act out/ draw/write what happens next after the end of the story/ book.
- Create a storyboard for a graphic novel analyzing the causes and effects of the content.
- Take the role of the answer to a math problem. Explain to a student the steps to use to solve the problem.
- Design a crossword puzzle using the vocabulary.

◆ Research a topic or person and create a comparison chart of the characteristics you have in common with the person or topic you are researching.

I'm often asked, "Does choice mean I have to let my students do whatever they want?" Notice that in each of the examples I have given, choice was balanced with structure. The activities provide choice within parameters that reflect the adult world. In most situations, you are asked to choose from options, whether it is purchasing a car or deciding on a job. When I work with graduate students, I tend to allow more flexibility with their options, but even then, I provide limits. If a graduate student wants to pursue a topic for a project, and it isn't one that I've recommended, I think *Does It Count?*, using a set of guidelines.

⇨ *Does It Count?*

C—Connected to the topic
O—On an appropriate level (not too easy, not too hard)
U—Understandable to you as the teacher
N—Not a repeat of earlier work
T—Thought-provoking

Perspectives

Lindsay Yearta used debates to teach her students to see different perspectives on an issue. She began with a handout, which included a statement: I am for/against (insert topic here). Next, she

assigned each child a position (for/against). Students then circled their position on the paper and then researched three reasons to support their position. They got into their groups and came up with what they thought the other group would say—what do you think their points are going to be? Then their task was to write down at least three points their opposition was going to have and think of/research comebacks to the opposition's points. So they had to think ahead, not only research their position but research the other side's position as well. Then when we held our debate, each student had to speak at least once.

Many middle and high school teachers I meet use a similar strategy when debating issues. A high school teacher in Wyoming asked his students to vote on two sides of an issue. Then each group was asked to research the opposing position. Students had the opportunity to change their position on the issue after the research. Finally, student teams debated the issue, with a deeper understanding of both sides. You'll see another application of this in the next section.

RAFT Strategy

Perhaps you would like your students to write a paragraph about the solar system (the topic you have been teaching in class). That is a fairly standard, low-level assignment that requires students to restate or summarize the information covered. Let's ratchet up the rigor using the RAFT strategy (Santa, Havens, & Macumber, 1996). RAFT stands for Role/Audience/Format/Topic. Using this strategy, students assume a role, such as an astronaut, and write from that perspective to a more authentic audience, such as people reading the astronaut's online blog. In this case, students are actually required to understand the topic at a higher level in order to complete the task.

⇨ *RAFT Examples*

Role	Audience	Format	Topic
An endangered species	Taxpayers	Public Facebook page	Asking support for the species' preservation
Minor character	Main character	Campaign speech or video	Asking for increased role in book/story
President	American people	Inaugural speech	Describing agenda for improving the country
Square root	Whole number	Love letter	Explaining current relationship
Berlin Wall	Future people interested in history	Timeline with tweets or comments	For 3 months prior to and after the fall of the Berlin Wall, telling what people said as they came to the wall/location
Diseased organ	Healthy organ	Instruction manual	Describing how to prevent disease
Job seeker	Human resources director	Cover letter and résumé	Applying for job

Missy Miles uses RAFT with her students, as she describes below:

When teaching students to look at things from multiple perspectives, I often start with a RAFT activity. I ask the students to write a letter to their parents, asking them to consider bending a rule (extending curfew, letting them go to the mall on the weekends with friends, etc. . . .). Then I have them reply to their own letter, this time playing the role of their parent. They have to think of a realistic reply they might get from their parent and include at least two logical reasons for either granting their wish or denying their request. Students have a very hard time doing this at first. I may also take controversial issues that really involve them and ask them to do the same thing.

For example, I may ask them to brainstorm the pros and cons of wearing school uniforms. Most students begin adamantly with the cons list, but I require that their lists be equally long (or short). So for every con, they are forced to come up with an advantage. I repeatedly have students tell me that they never realized how many arguments there are for the other side. I usually culminate this mini unit with a research project. They have to choose another controversial issue and research both sides—no matter how biased they are going into it. Then they must write a persuasive paper arguing for the side they didn't originally favor. I say originally because, once again, I have many students who tell me that the process made them change their minds completely. When I get these comments, I know they have learned how to look at different perspectives of an issue!

Thinking Hats

Another way to help students think about a topic from a variety of perspectives is through the use of Thinking Hats (DeBono, 1999). The process provides six different ways of viewing or discussing information and is helpful anytime you want students to look at something through different lenses.

⇨ Six Thinking Hats

The White Hat	calls for information known or needed. "The facts, just the facts."
The Yellow Hat	symbolizes brightness and optimism. Under this hat, you explore the positives and probe for value and benefit
The Black Hat	judgment—the devil's advocate or why something may not work. Spot the difficulties and dangers, where things might go wrong. Probably the most powerful and useful of the hats but a problem if overused.
The Red Hat	signifies feelings, hunches, and intuition. When using this hat, you can express emotions and feelings and share fears, likes, dislikes, loves, and hates.
The Green Hat	focuses on creativity; the possibilities, alternatives, and new ideas. It's an opportunity to express new concepts and new perceptions.
The Blue Hat	is used to manage the thinking process. It's the control mechanism that ensures the Six Thinking Hats guidelines are observed.

Kendra Alston uses Thinking Hats to help in the brainstorming process of argumentative (problem/solution) writing.

> The students had to think of a problem and used the Thinking Hats strategy as a way to help them elaborate or support their solutions or perspectives and as a way to organize their essays. We also used it in class meetings as a type of conflict resolution strategy.

You could also use Thinking Hats in debates to connect thinking and speaking. Helping your students view the information you are teaching from different perspectives does not have to be difficult or time-consuming. You can integrate these simple activities into your existing lessons and, in the process, increase the level of engagement by your students.

Connections

Within lessons, students need to understand how to connect what they are learning. There are three types of connections you can help students make: text to self, text to text, and text to world. You can also substitute the word *learning* for *text*.

Text to Self

The first connection most students make is to themselves. As you teach, encourage them to explain how what they are learning connects to their individual lives. As students relate their own experiences to the material, their learning increases. There are several prompting questions you can use to discuss text-to-self connections.

⇒ *Text-to-Self Connection Prompts*

This reminds me of . . .
I like (or don't like) . . .
I know about . . .
I feel (what emotion does the text prompt?) . . .

Text to Text

Every time you introduce a text to students, whether it is a book, an article, or even a word, it's important to connect it to other texts they have read. I was in an elementary classroom where the teacher had a huge bulletin board at the front of the room. Students had drawn book covers for all the books and other texts they had read. Whenever the class read a new book, the teacher posted a cover, and students used string to connect the new book with any other books that were related. The class created a visual web of connections for everyone to see.

I found I needed to encourage my social studies students to think deeper about those connections. For example, if we read about historical documents, they thought they were finished.

But I wanted them to also remember the actual primary source of that document. Especially at the beginning of the year, you'll need to provide more support and guiding questions to help your students make those connections.

⇨ *Text-to-Text Connection Guide*

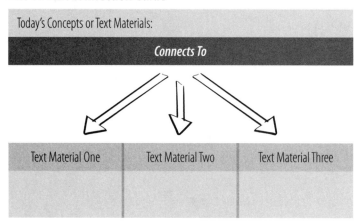

Text to World

Finally, you want your students to connect with the world around them. How does what they are reading or learning link to something else they know or have heard about? Missy Miles incorporates text-to-world connections through readings of current events. Her fifth graders read news articles and follow up by making two-minute oral presentations to the class. In addition to summarizing the event, they must explain how it affects them or someone they know. Students enjoy the activity, called "Keeping US Current!"

Conclusion

Opening the focus of your instruction allows students to take ownership of instruction and apply their creativity to learning. There is also an array of the level of open-endedness in your lessons, ranging from more structured to less structured.

:Q: Points to Ponder

Use the following sentence starters to reflect on the chapter.

I learned . . .

I'd like to try . . .

I need . . .

I'd like to share something from this chapter with . . .

6

Raise Expectations

The final strategy for increasing rigor is to raise expectations in your classroom. In *The Art and Science of Teaching*, Robert J. Marzano describes actions that are representative of lowered expectations. He compares teachers' behaviors toward high-achieving and low-achieving students. As he points out, teachers often exhibit different actions with students who are low achieving. These actions include less attention, less wait time, fewer opportunities to answer, less feedback and follow-up, and fewer positive interactions, such as eye contact, praise, and nonverbal cues (Marzano, 2007, ASCD). In this chapter, we'll look at your expectations and your students' expectations.

Raise Expectations

Student Motivation
Beliefs and Actions
Ensuring Rigor for EACH Student
Celebrating Progress

Student Motivation

One critical aspect of rigor is student motivation. You may have heard that "rigor and relevance" or "rigor, relevance, and relationships" are important. They are. I tend to address relationships and relevance when I talk about student motivation.

Relationships

First, we always have a relationship with our students. However, it's up to us to decide if it is positive or negative. I recently talked to a teacher who said, "I don't have time to get to know all my students. My job is to teach my content." I respect his perspective, but I don't agree. I believe all teachers teach students—they just differ in the content they teach. I also believe in the old adage, "They don't care how much you know until they know how much you care." At the beginning of the school year, my son said he hoped his teachers would stop and learn about the students before they started giving homework and focusing so much on the content.

If you plan to increase rigor in your classroom, you'll need to tap into your students' motivations, and building a relationship is the first step. There are several ways you can get to know your students. It's as simple as asking them questions, taking time to listen and notice what they are doing, or giving them an opportunity to creatively describe themselves.

For example, you can have students tell you about their dreams for the future. You might do this through writing, technology, or another outlet. Kendra Alston has her students choose or write a theme song for their lives. Sarah Ehrman, who teaches in a high school in Los Angeles, says,

> My first assignment is [to ask students to write an] autobiography. It must be three typed pages, anything about themselves. Everyone wants a chance to tell their story: where they were born, about their family. They can tell me "I have a bad home situation" or "I work long hours." They write about a sport, extracurricular activities, anything they want. They are motivated when they think you want to know about them. When I started my first job, it was because the other teacher quit (it was an inner-city school teaching the "troubled" kids). They had 15 subs before I came, and they knew they were "bad kids." One of the students told other teachers

[they] were so surprised that I cared enough to have them write three pages and that I cared enough to read it. I did not know that would be a big deal, but it was.

Sylvia White at Reid Ross Classical School asks her students to wear their dreams. As a follow-up to a discussion of Martin Luther King Jr.'s life and his dream for all people, her students design shirts. On the front, they illustrate their dream using fabric paints, computer design graphics, or any type of embroidery. On the back, students write the steps to achieving their goal, which is based on their own research. It is an excellent way for students to learn the next steps required to achieving their goals.

Value and Success

Do you teach students who are intrinsically motivated? Intrinsic motivation comes from within. It's the sense of working toward something simply because we want to or because we see value in the accomplishment. It is relatively easy to know when a student is intrinsically motivated.

⇨ Indicators of a Student's Intrinsic Motivation

He or she

- ◆ pursues the activity independently;
- ◆ enjoys the activity;
- ◆ wants to work through completion;
- ◆ moves beyond the minimum expectations;
- ◆ is motivated by the task or the learning, not rewards.

In schools, we focus much of our time and attention on extrinsic rewards, such as points and prizes, because they are easier to deal with and they do motivate many students, particularly for the short-term. Intrinsic motivation, on the other hand, seems to be harder for us. After all, how do you motivate someone to be self-motivated? Let's take a look at some strategies that can help.

Foundational Elements

Intrinsic motivation has two foundational elements: people are more motivated when they value what they are doing and when they believe they have a chance for success. Teachers can create a learning environment that supports both components.

Value. First, students are more likely to be intrinsically motivated to learn if they value what they are asked to do. Although educators frequently talk about rigor and relevance, value includes relevance and more. Even though it is important for students to see the relevance of learning, sometimes students connect with instruction because they enjoy the class or have a positive relationship with the teacher. There are five ways to add value to your classroom.

⇨ *Ways to Add Value to Instruction*

V	Variety	Include a variety of activities, assignments, projects, etc. Have a structure, but don't get caught up in a boring routine.
A	Attractiveness	Integrate elements of movement, curiosity, and originality into your lessons.
L	Locus of control	To address students' need for some control over their circumstances or ownership in the learning, provide opportunities for them to be a part of the learning experience, rather than simply being told what to do.
U	Utility	Students need to see the utility, purpose, or the relevance of the lesson. Provide real-life connections.
E	Enjoyment	Students are more motivated when they find pleasure in what they are doing. Although you need to have a classroom with structure and order, that may "look" different in different classrooms. It is absolutely, positively OK to smile and have fun. Play games, make jokes, and do something different.

Building Blocks for Achieving Success. Students are also motivated when they believe they have a chance to be successful. Too often, we have students who have never been successful in a school setting. Students need to set and achieve goals in order to build a sense of confidence, which leads to a willingness to try something else, which in turn begins a cycle that leads to higher levels of success. Success leads to success, and the achievements of small goals are building blocks to success at larger goals.

Success Cycle

Part of raising expectations is to help students believe they can be successful. There are many ways you can build students' confidence in themselves.

⇨ *Ways to Build Confidence*

Provide questions or assignments that are open-ended and for which there are no wrong answers. This also provides another opportunity to get to know each student.

Provide additional support during lessons, such as graphic organizers, learning guides, etc. (See Chapter 4: Give Appropriate Support and Guidance for more examples.)

Use multiple intelligences activities linked to students' strengths.

Encourage students and provide feedback and praise that reinforce their efforts, not just the final product.

Beliefs and Actions

I'd like you to think about several questions as we move into a tough topic—our beliefs and actions.

⇨ *Reflection Questions*

- ◆ Who is your worst student this year?
- ◆ Who was your worst student last year?
- ◆ What do you believe about student learning?
- ◆ Do all your students have the potential to learn?
- ◆ Do they learn because of you or in spite of you?

As you reflect, I'm not looking for the standard, pat answer: "I believe all students can learn." When you truly reflect on where you are as a teacher and how your actions reflect your beliefs, what is your answer? We know we should all have high expectations for each student every moment of every day. But in reality, that is very difficult.

Just as butterflies are not in their final beautiful state when they hatch or when they are caterpillars or when they form into a chrysalis, so our students are not in their completed state when we are teaching them.

Now go back to those original questions. Where are the students you teach? Are they caterpillars? Or are they inside a chrysalis? What does that mean to you? If you think about your students as "butterflies-in-the-making," how does that change how you view them? One of the most difficult things for us to do as teachers is to keep our expectations high, especially when our students' actions make us think less of them.

This was especially true for me with Daniel. Before I met him, 23 teachers came to see me to tell me how sorry they were that I would have him in class. I'm ashamed to admit to you that this shaded my perspective of him. I was nice to him, but I was always waiting for him to disrupt class. After all, he had done so many bad things in other classes. By the end of the year, I gave Daniel a D for the class because I could not bear to teach him again. And since I taught remedial students, it was likely I would have him in class if he stayed behind a grade.

The next year, my principal moved me to eighth grade, and—you guessed it—I had Daniel again. That day I realized I was treating him as if I expected trouble, and I vowed to stop. I met with him, said I would like a clean slate, and suggested we forget about last year. I then told him I was convinced he could earn a B in my class and that I would do everything I could to support him.

That year, I checked in at the beginning of class to ensure he had materials, made sure to praise him when he succeeded, and encouraged him when he was struggling. In short, I treated him as I did all my other students. He changed from a troublemaker to a positive leader in the class and earned a B at the end of the year.

Sadly, a year and a half later, he was expelled from the high school. I had moved for a different job, but when I returned to visit, I learned of the incident from his aunt. I said to her, "What really happened? I'm sure he didn't bring a gun to school." Through her tears, she replied,

> You are the only one who didn't assume he was guilty. He took a gun away from another student who planned to shoot someone, but then he put it in his locker. He said if you had still been at the junior high, he would have called you but that no one else would believe him.

Daniel is my ever-present reminder of the power of our expectations. Realistically, I wasted an entire year of his life in seventh grade. And the only things that changed during his successful year were my expectations for him and my actions that reflected my changed perspective.

There are always days when students challenge us to come up with any positive thoughts about them, but those are the days they need us the most. They need us to believe they are butterflies when they are most acting like caterpillars! Unfortunately, we sometimes fall into the trap of expecting less of some students than others. Just as it happened to me with Daniel, it can happen to all of us in subtle ways, especially when we don't actively reflect on our beliefs and actions.

What is the best way to ensure our expectations and beliefs are high? It's through our actions. Are we using positive statements rather than negative ones? Are we providing appropriate wait time or do we send the message that we don't really think students will be able to answer? A participant in one of my workshops shared her experience with a mismatch between her actions and beliefs. As she explained,

> I have always believed in and had high expectations for my students. I also knew that I provided the best support possible for them to be successful. One day, one of my students had a question after class. This is a student who always has a question after class. I was listening, but I was also scanning the hall for potential problems. He finally said in a loud voice, "Will you at least look at me when I'm asking for help?" That's the day I realized that even though I believed in providing the best support for students, I didn't always act in ways that reflected my belief to students. Balancing duties will always be an issue, but that day I realized sometimes my frustration gets the best of me.

How are you doing with high expectations? Take a look at the self-assessment chart that follows to help you reflect.

⇨ *Self-Assessment Chart*

	I'm confident I'm in good shape here.	Sometimes this is good, sometimes not.	I need to think about how I can improve.
I truly believe all students can learn.			
I never think "this student is never going to learn this."			
I insist that each student learns, and I don't stop until he or she does.			
I ignore or stop teachers when they start telling negative stories about students.			
When I'm in a meeting with other teachers, and we are given an opportunity to share, I tell a positive story about my students, even when I've had a bad week.			
I take time every day to write down at least three positive things about my students.			
I recognize students' efforts, not just their successes.			
I say more positive things than negative ones.			

In a journal or on separate paper, add examples to support your choices.

Ensuring Rigor for EACH Student

When I was working with focus groups of teachers to refine my original, research-based definition, they all agreed on one change—use EACH student, not ALL students. Their comments were about how the definition must be individualized; if we say *all* students, some get lost; and do we really look at each student, or do we look at the class?

Ongoing Opportunities

As you think about your own classroom, there are probably plenty of times you can create options for your students to demonstrate their understanding during the lesson. For example, I regularly visit classrooms where teachers use the think-pair-share approach, asking students to think about an answer to a question, then pair up and share ideas.

As I mentioned earlier, other options include students responding by holding up white boards or with thumbs up or down. If you have available technology, the use of clickers or other immediate response tools is motivating. I've also seen teachers effectively use text messaging and Twitter to engage students throughout the lesson. The issue is not whether the tool is high or low tech; the question is, "Does it work?"

Those are quick, easy-to-use assessments to check for understanding at key points within a lesson. There are also other participation techniques that involve every student.

Groups

Carie Hucks capitalizes on her middle school students' desire to socialize.

I try to incorporate sharing into every lesson with my students. A trick I use is a colored die. I post questions specific to a lesson in the room and match the question with a number 1–6. I give each group of students a die.

They take turns rolling the die and respond based on the number rolled. The novelty of being able to roll a die helps engage my students in the lesson more effectively than just giving them questions and asking them to discuss.

You can also ask students to form small groups and discuss what they have read. My son's science teacher in the sixth grade asked groups of students to create raps for their section of the chapter. It was engaging, motivating, and required every student to participate.

You may need to teach students how to appropriately participate in groups. Give them your expectations for effective group work. The following list provides some examples. You may also wish to put your expectations into a rubric, to teach students cooperative learning skills and to assess their progress.

⇨ Sample Expectations for Effective Group Work

You're a Team Player if . . .

♦ You listen respectfully to other team members and offer suggestions that help the group.
♦ You are engaged and on-task, looking for ways to help the group complete the project.
♦ If someone needs help, you encourage (positive words) rather than criticize (negative words).
♦ You give all your attention to the activity to help your group achieve its goals.

Question Starters

Another way to ensure understanding is to ask students to create their own questions. Students can work in pairs or small groups and make up questions about a story they have read or review for a test. I found that, especially at the beginning of the year, my students struggled with the open-ended nature of that activity. It seemed they needed a bit more support, so I made sets of question-starter cards. Students could draw a card and use the starter word or phrase to create their own questions. That extra bit of support was very helpful. Then, as the year progressed, they were able to craft high-level questions without any prompting from me or the cards.

⇨ Sample Question Starters

Which event . . .
Why did . . .
If . . .
How might . . .
Where did . . .
Which word or phrase . . .
What connection . . .

Grand Conversations

Connie Forrester describes one of her favorite activities: "Grand Conversations." She teaches kindergarten, but the concept, similar to Socratic Circles, is applicable across all grade levels. Listen to her describe her particular use of the method.

I would usually introduce this strategy in October during our unit of study on nonfiction. To introduce the strategy, I would ask the children if they knew what the word *conversation* meant. After some discussion, one child would usually come up with the fact that conversation is talking. I would go on to tell the children that "Grand Conversations" are one strategy that the big kids use when they talk about books. I would explain the ground rules to the children. You would be amazed how quickly the children catch on and how much they enjoy this strategy. They would beg to use it after we had read a book. However, I found "Grand Conversations" worked best when used after a nonfiction text.

⇒ *Ground Rules for "Grand Conversations"*

- ◆ One person talks at a time.
- ◆ When you respond to a classmate, you make a comment, ask a question, or make a connection. Your response must match the previous person's train of thought. (For instance, if we are having a conversation about a spider's habitat and the next child begins discussing what he had for dinner last night, the first child can pick someone else.)
- ◆ No one raises his or her hand. I explain to the children that when people have conversations, no one raises their hands. (We would either toss a beach ball to the person to talk or the child would sit up very straight to be recognized.)

Celebrating Progress

One of the most important ways you can demonstrate high expectations as well as help your students raise their expectations of themselves is to celebrate progress as well as achievement.

In today's schools, we tend to focus on whether students have achieved a certain standard or goal. That's great, but there are some students for whom that is an impossible benchmark. I used to joke with my students that they couldn't see past the end of their noses to look at our long-term goals (especially the year-end standardized test). If you plan to help your students achieve, you'll need to celebrate each step they make toward the goal.

One way to do this is to have a "Progress Is Power" bulletin board where you can track students' improvements and showcase the progress they are making. In the classrooms I've visited, teachers use anything from train tracks to balloons to graphs to visually represent the progress of their students. I'd offer one caution, though. Make sure the emphasis is on individual progress, not on competing with others.

How we praise or reinforce students can also make a difference. This is particularly important for those students who do not understand the importance of their own efforts. I recently heard about a study (*The New York Times*, 1998) that looked at the differences in praising students for their ability versus praising their effort. Perhaps surprisingly, those students who were continually told how smart they were began to underachieve over time. Those who were praised for their efforts began to try harder and achieved more. Take a look back at page 55 for related points.

I saw this in my own classroom. Ronita, one of my students, generally struggled in class. One day, after a lot of hard work and studying, she made an A on a project. I was so proud of her but was stunned at her response. First, she thanked me for "giving" her an A. When I told her she earned the grade, she smiled and said, "It's my lucky day."

She did not realize that effort does make a difference. She thought achievement was due to an outside force, such as my help or luck. For students like Ronita, reinforcing effort leads to later success and teaches them the value of their own efforts. And for high-achieving students who are always told how smart they are, the lack of praise for effort teaches them they don't have to work hard—"I'm just so smart, I can ace this without any work."

Finally, share with students stories about people and their dreams and goals for their lives. It's important to talk about men and women who achieved their dreams despite failures. By continually showing your students how other people accomplished their goals, you broaden their visions for their own lives. It's easy to find the stories; a simple Google search may provide you with what you need. Ideally, find examples appropriate to your subject area and the ages of your students.

⇨ *Books With Stories of Successful People Who Have Overcome Failure*

The Secret of Success Is Not a Secret: Stories of Famous People Who Persevered, by Darcy Andries
Great Failures of the Extremely Successful, by Steve Young
Unstoppable, by Cynthia Kersey
Staying With It: Role Models of Perseverance, by Emerson Klees
The Road to Success Is Paved With Failure : How Hundreds of Famous People Triumphed Over Inauspicious Beginnings, Crushing Rejection, Humiliating Defeats and Other Speed Bumps Along Life's Highway, by Joey Green

Conclusion

Raising our expectations for student learning is more than our words; it's the actions we take to reinforce the raised expectations and the support we provide to help students move to higher levels of learning. This is not necessarily a quick or an easy process, but it is one of the cornerstones of rigor.

☼ Points to Ponder

Use the following sentence starters to reflect on the chapter.

I learned . . .

I'd like to try . . .

I need . . .

I'd like to share something from this chapter with . . .

7

Challenges and Adventures

As we finish our discussion about rigor, let's take a look at five challenges that can be either stumbling blocks or stepping stones in your journey.

Challenges and Adventures

I'm Just Not Sure
I Don't Know Where to Start
I Don't Have Enough Time, Support, or Resources
I'm Facing Resistance
What About Grading and Assessment?

I'm Just Not Sure

You may have conflicting feelings about increasing rigor in your classroom. If so, you may be concerned because you don't see the value in the change or you aren't sure how successful the change will be.

The Southwest Educational Development Lab created a way of monitoring change efforts. The Concerns-Based Adoption Model (CBAM) (Hord, Rutherford, Huling-Austin, & Hall, 1987) helps you understand what occurs when a school moves from implementing a change, such as increasing rigor, to institutionalizing that change.

The authors created the CBAM model and identified seven stages of concern. It recognizes that change is complex and that people experience changes individually from minimal awareness of the innovation to identifying ways to improve on the innovation.

Stages of Concern	Examples of Expression of Concern
6 Refocusing	What else can I do to improve rigor? How can I make my classroom even more rigorous?
5 Collaboration	I'm pleased with my effort to improve rigor, but what have others done?
4 Consequence	Now that I've increased rigor, how am I doing? What evidence do I have that it is helping my students?
3 Management	How can I develop the skills to create a more rigorous classroom? How can I do this with everything else I have to do?
2 Personal	How will increasing rigor impact me? What will my plan to improve rigor look like?
1 Informational	How can I increase rigor in my classroom? Where do I get information?
0 Awareness	What is rigor? Things are fine; I'm not concerned about it.

Adapted from Hord, Rutherford, Huling-Austin, & Hall, 1987

Personal concerns (awareness, informational, personal) often characterize your first steps. As you begin to launch your plans, management concerns emerge. Then, once you are under way, you will focus on the effects of rigor on students and on their classrooms. Individuals progress through the stages in a developmental manner. Everyone will not move at the same pace or have the same intensity of feeling. Don't worry; that's normal!

I Don't Know Where to Start

Ideally, you could snap your fingers, and all your students would immediately embrace more rigorous expectations and assignments. Creating an environment in which each student is expected to learn at high levels, each student is supported so he or she can learn at high levels, and each student demonstrates learning at high levels usually takes consistency and persistence. However, there are concrete steps you can take to make the road to rigor easier.

Your first step is to have a vision of your classroom where all those things occur. Write a vision letter. Imagine it's the end of the year, and your classroom was truly rigorous and engaging. Take your time to think about what you already do and how you will improve and grow. Describe fully how things have changed now that each student you teach learns at high levels. What did you do to fully support each student to reach those high levels? Add as many details as possible. Then read it at least once a week. Clarifying and focusing on your vision is the foundation for your success.

Second, decide on three specific steps you will take to increase rigor in your classroom. We've discussed a variety of strategies, but consider what you already use in your classroom. How can you make those strategies or activities more rigorous? As you incorporate the new ideas, take time to reflect and make any adaptations. No idea is perfect; most will need some adjustments to be effective with your students. Then continue to incorporate at least one new strategy or idea each week throughout the school year. As you slowly integrate changes into your instruction, you will create the vision you described in your letter.

I Don't Have Enough Time, Support, or Resources

Once you decide to add more rigor to your classroom, you are likely to encounter three obstacles. First, there doesn't seem to be time to add one more thing to your schedule. It takes time to plan, implement, reflect, and adjust. Where can you find the time and energy?

The issue is how to be both more efficient and more effective. The best approach is to prioritize what you are doing. This is very difficult because you have multiple priorities, some more urgent than others. It's also important to recognize that rigor is not "one more thing." It's interrelated to your efforts to improve student motivation, increase student engagement, implement new standards, and differentiate your instruction. Combine your efforts to streamline your time.

I believe the key to improving rigor is what goes on in each classroom. It is the curricular, instructional, and assessment practices you use. Momentum in the classroom can be maintained even in the face of competing pressures. However, you do still have some control of what you do in your classroom. It is possible to add the instructional practices I've suggested even when you are preparing for formal assessments or other priorities.

Second, you may not believe you have support from parents, other teachers, or school leaders. It is more difficult when you feel like you are the only one trying to increase rigor. Remember to focus on actions within your control until you can garner more support. Also, most of the stakeholder groups I mentioned may need more information or time to embrace your efforts. We'll look more at this issue in the next section: I'm Facing Resistance.

Third, you may also feel you don't have the resources you need. These are challenging times for schools, and the reality is that you may not be able to obtain the resources you need. Because of that, I've chosen to include activities that do not require a high level of funding to implement. If you have technology in your classroom, these strategies are easily adaptable. Finally, take advantage of free resources on the Internet.

I'm Facing Resistance

Although it's not a certainty, you may meet some resistance from students, parents, teachers, and administrators as you increase the rigor in your classroom. Let's take a look at each.

Students

There are several reasons students may be resistant. Some students simply don't see the value of hard work. Others don't feel successful in school, and the thought of something that is even more difficult increases their fears of failure. While I can't solve every problem you face with your students, here are three recommendations that will help ease the transition to more rigorous work.

First, recognize the source of the resistance. The value and success aspects of motivation impact students in more ways than you may realize. As you create your lessons, tap into value from your students' perspective. In the early stages of planning, ask yourself "What will I say to a student who says, 'What's in it for me?'" Integrate real-world applications as much as possible. In order to help students feel successful, build in multiple opportunities for appropriate scaffolding and support.

Next, give your students time. Real change doesn't happen overnight. If your students grumble and complain, minimize the discussion, increase your focus on relevance and success, and keep moving forward. Celebrate their successes, large and small. Include positive reinforcement for reaching goals but also for sustained effort toward a goal. Focus on the long-term effects of helping your students grow, and you will see a difference. And remember, it will probably take longer than you'd prefer, and your students won't always tell you they appreciate what you do.

Finally, although you need to be clear about what you are doing, don't give rigor too much of the spotlight. I talked with one teacher who said, "When I created lessons that were highly interactive and engaging, I made sure I incorporated the relevance for students and showed them I would help them be successful, they quit complaining and realized this was just about learning!" Expect the best from your students, create the best lessons to ensure learning, provide appropriate support for every student, and don't apologize for your high standards.

Parents

In addition to providing information for your students, you need to communicate effectively with parents. It's important to provide a clear description of what you expect. If your expectations are higher than other teachers' expectations, or if this is a new concept for parents, you will need to focus on your rationale and the benefits of rigor. It's certainly easier if everyone in your school is collaborating as you increase expectations, but if that isn't the case, then you simply need to ensure that parents understand why your requirements are different. Think about the two keys of motivation. Parents need to see value in what you are doing, and they need to feel their sons or daughters will be successful.

⇒ Formula for Communication

Value + Success = Understanding

I suggest you share information throughout the year. You can continue to use newsletters or e-mails, but shift the focus to celebrating the progress students are making. You can take digital pictures of their writing or projects they have created. Incorporate their reflective comments about learning, using their comments to showcase growth. This can also help you balance an overemphasis on grades.

Teachers

Unfortunately, as you incorporate new ideas in your classroom, you may also meet resistance from other teachers in your school. I think this is probably the most difficult challenge in terms of resistance. You hope other teachers will support you. But if you find that is not the case, there are two actions you can take to help you balance the negative criticism.

First, try to keep a low profile. Many new teachers tell me that when they share "too much," other teachers may be turned off or even threatened. Share with other teachers, ask for help, and even invite them into your classroom, but if you feel you are hitting a wall of resistance, take a step back.

Next, seek out other teachers with similar beliefs. One of the benefits of the graduate program at my former university is the support and friendship of other teachers. At graduation, I was regularly told by my students that one of the things they would miss most was the ability to come in and discuss issues with others who shared similar perspectives about making a difference for students. It's easy to feel isolated when you are trying something new; find others who can support you. One excellent way to connect with other teachers is through the use of technology, such as Twitter and online bulletin boards at teacher-oriented sites.

Finally, remember your focus. One teacher told me, "High performance often leads to jealousy in the workplace. I suppose that's anywhere, except that in teaching it should be about the students." I agree. It is about the students. When you center your effort and attention on what is best for your students, it helps you balance the criticism from others. One of the most effective ways to keep yourself motivated in tough times is to keep a daily list of five positive things that happen with your students. Then, when you have a bad day, you can look back at the list to help you remember that you are making a difference.

Administrators

At times, teachers are concerned their administrators won't support them. For example, in one of my recent workshops, a teacher came up after the session with a question. "Are you sure the activities we did are rigorous? I did one of them last week during an observation, and my principal said it wasn't rigorous."

My best recommendation in that situation was information. I suggested she go back to her principal and simply show her the activities we did, and the excerpt from my book where I explained the rationale for the strategy. I also recommended she ask, in a nonconfrontational manner, for more feedback on her lesson.

I later received an e-mail from the teacher. She said the conversation with her principal was very successful, and at the end, they both agreed that the lesson was rigorous. Sometimes, you may simply need to share and discuss information in order to reach consensus.

Other times, you can encounter resistance without understanding why. I suggest using the same strategies I recommend for students and parents. Try to understand the resistance, considering value and success. Share your successes at appropriate times, and keep the channels of communication open.

What About Grading and Assessment?

I've found that nothing derails attempts at rigor as quickly as problems with grading. Yet before we talk about grades, we should discuss the aspect of assessment that can have a greater impact on student learning, formative assessment.

Using Formative Assessment to Fuel Your Instruction

Throughout this book, I have placed emphasis on what you can do in your classroom. In *Literacy from A to Z* (2008),

I describe formative assessment as a three-step process: look at your students to learn about them, watch their progress, and help them grow.

⇨ Three-Step Process of Formative Assessment

1. Look at your students to learn about them.
2. Watch their progress.
3. Help them grow.

There are many ways you can gather data and use it to design instruction. We will not take the time to fully investigate formative assessment; that would take an entire book. For our purposes, simply recognize that the instructional strategies described throughout this book are excellent ways to determine if your students are learning.

That is the critical difference with formative assessment. Its main purpose is to *help your students GROW.*

⇨ Help Students GROW

G—Gauge where your students are.
R—Recognize their strengths and weaknesses.
O—One step at a time, provide instruction to help them grow.
W—Watch them rise to higher levels.

Grading

As I said, some of the greatest resistance from students, parents, and other teachers usually arises around grading practices, assigning grades for student work. It's one of the most controversial issues related to increasing rigor. A teacher once told me, "The only thing my students and their parents care about is an A."

There are many purposes for grading, including communicating achievement status, grouping students, and providing an extrinsic motivator for students. There is no perfect way to grade. But there are steps you can take to minimize the negative aspects of grading.

Grading is an important topic, especially when you work to increase rigor. It deserves more attention than I can provide here, but in *Rigor Is Not a Four-Letter Word* (2008), I identified six ways to minimize the negative aspects of grading.

⇨ Minimize Negative Aspects of Grading

- ◆ Recognize the value of grading to students, families, and others.
- ◆ Shift the emphasis to learning.
- ◆ Provide clear guidelines.
- ◆ Require quality work.
- ◆ Communicate clearly.
- ◆ Be patient.

The first is to recognize that grades are of value to students, families, and others. It may be for college admission or for affirmation of their worth. Regardless, grades are important.

It is also important to shift the emphasis to learning, not just grades. This is not easy and takes time. Students and their families will probably never ignore grades completely, but you can begin by working with teachers to shift the emphasis to student learning.

Providing clear guidelines and a clear rubric for all projects and key assignments is also important. Many students don't know what "good" looks like, and then teachers become frustrated when quality work is not produced.

Use of a "Not Yet" grading scale for projects and assignments shifts the emphasis to learning and allows students to revise and resubmit work until it is at an acceptable level. Requiring quality work, work that meets your expectations, lets students know you value learning, not just completion of an assignment.

Be sure to communicate your expectations clearly. Students and families need to know school and classroom practices for grades. They need to know about homework and what happens if it is not completed. I often find schools where teachers are asked to provide a written grading policy so their procedures are clear.

Finally, be patient. For most schools, grading is a reality we must live with. It takes time to change practices and for teachers to gain confidence with a new approach to grading. As with students, the "Not Yet" grading policy applies to you and your work to deal with grading and rigor in your school.

Conclusion

As you begin to increase rigor in your classroom, you will likely find some challenges. Remember that increasing rigor is a journey, and although you may run into roadblocks, if you keep your focus, you will move past them to make progress. Don't give up! As Kevin, a student I interviewed, said, "Don't be discouraged if some of your students think it is hard because it is supposed to be hard." How true . . . and quite applicable to our journey.

☐ Points to Ponder

Use the following sentence starters to reflect on the chapter.

I learned . . .

I'd like to try . . .

I need . . .

I'd like to share something from this chapter with . . .

References

Ainsworth, L. (2010). Rigorous curriculum design. Englewood, CO: Advanced Learning Press.

Ainsworth, L. (2003). Power standards. Englewood, CO: Advanced Learning Press.

Allen, J. (2000). *Yellow brick roads: Shared and guided paths to independent reading.* Portland, ME: Stenhouse Publishers.

Allen, J. (2004). *Tools for teaching content literacy.* Portland, ME: Stenhouse Publishers.

Anderson, L. W., Krathwohl, D. R., Airasian, P. W., Cruikshank, K. A., Mayer, R. E., Pintrich, P. R., et al. (Eds.). (2001). *A taxonomy for learning, teaching, and assessing: A revision of Bloom's taxonomy of educational objectives.* New York, NY: Longman.

Black, P., Harrison, C., Lee, C., Marshall, B., & William, D. (2004). Working inside the black box: Assessment for learning in the classroom. *Phi Delta Kappan, 86,* pp. 9–21.

Blackburn, B. R. (2005). *Classroom motivation from A to Z: How to engage your students in learning.* Larchmont, NY: Eye On Education.

Blackburn, B. R. (2007). *Classroom instruction from A to Z: How to promote student learning.* Larchmont, NY: Eye On Education.

Blackburn, B. R. (2008). *Literacy from A to Z: Engaging students in reading, writing, speaking, & listening.* Larchmont, NY: Eye On Education.

Blackburn, B. R. (2008). *Rigor is not a four-letter word.* Larchmont, NY: Eye On Education.

Boston, C. (2002). The concept of formative assessment. *Practical Assessment, Research & Evaluation, 8*(9). Retrieved from http://PAREonline.net/getvn.asp?v=8&n=9

Carmichael, Sheila Byrd, Gabrielle Martino, Kathleen Porter-Magee, and W. Stephen Wilson. (July 21, 2010). *The State of State Standards—and the Common Core—in 2010.* Retrieved from Thomas B. Fordham Institute: Advancing Educational Excellence Web site: http://www.edexcellence.net/publications-issues/publications/the-state-of-state.html

Clark, R. (2003). *The essential 55: An award-winning educator's rules for discovering the successful student in every child.* New York, NY: Hyperion.

Costa, A. & Kallick, B. (2008). Learning and Leading with Habits of Mind: 16 Essential Characteristics for Success. Alexandria, VA: Association for Supervision and Curriculum Development.

Daniels, H., & Zemelman, S. (2004). *Subjects Matter: Every teacher's guide to content area reading.* Portsmouth, NH: Heinemann.

DeBono, E. (1999). *Six thinking hats.* New York, NY: Little, Brown and Company.

Deckers, L. (2005). *Motivation: biological, psychological, and environmental* (2nd ed.). Upper Saddle River, NJ: Pearson Education.

DuFour, Ri., DuFour, Re., Eaker, R. & Many, T. (2006). *Learning by doing: A handbook for professional learning communities at work.* Bloomington, IN: Solution Tree.

Erwin, J. C. (2004). *The classroom of choice: Giving students what they need and getting what you want.* Alexandria, VA: Association for Supervision and Curriculum Development.

Fielding, L., & Roller, C. (1992, May). Making difficult books accessible and easy books acceptable. *The Reading Teacher,* 678–685.

Guskey, T. R., & Bailey, J. M. (2001). *Developing grading and reporting systems for student learning.* Thousand Oaks, CA: Corwin Press.

Hord, S., Rutherford, W., Hurling-Austin, L. & Hall, G. (1987). Taking charge of change. Alexandria, VA: Association of Supervision and Curriculum Development.

Kersey, C. (2005) Unstoppable. Naperville, IL: Sourcebooks, Inc.

Larkin, M. (2001). *Providing support for student independence through scaffolded instruction.* Teaching Exceptional Children, *34,* 30–34.

Marzano, R. J., Pickering, D. J., & Pollock, J. E. (2001). *Classroom instruction that works: Research-based strategies for increasing student achievement.* Alexandria, VA: Association for Supervision and Curriculum Development.

Marzano, R. J. (2007). *The art and science of teaching: A comprehensive framework for effective instruction.* Alexandria, VA: Association for Supervision and Curriculum Development.

Marzano, R. J. (2011). The perils and promises of discovery learning. *Educational Leadership.* 69: 1. (86–87).

Metametrics. (n.d.). *The 3 R's: Using the Lexile Framework.* Durham, NC: Author.

National Governor's Association and Council of Chief State School Officers. (2010). *The common core state standards.* Author.

The National Governors Association Center for Best Practices and The Council of Chief State School Officers. About the Standards. In *Common Core State Standards Initiative: Preparing America's Students for College & Career.* Retrieved March 7, 2011, from http://www.corestandards.org/about-the-standards.

The New York Times. (July 14, 1998) Praise children for effort, not intelligence, study says. http://www.nytimes.com/1998/07/14/science/praise-children-for-effort-not-intelligence-study-says.html

Popham, W. J. (2008). *Transformative assessment*. Alexandria, VA: Association for Supervision and Curriculum Development.

Reeves, D. B. (2003). *Making standards work: How to implement standards-based assessments in the classroom, school, and district*. Englewood, CO: Advanced Learning Press.

Santa, C., Havens, L., & Macumber, E. (1996). *Creating independence through student-owned strategies*. Dubuque, IA: Kendall/Hunt.

Southern Regional Education Board (SREB) (2004). *Literacy across the curriculum: Setting and implementing goals for grades six through twelve* (Site Development Guide No. 12). Atlanta, GA: Author.

Strong, R. W., Silver, H. F., & Perrini, M. J. (2001). *Teaching what matters most: Standards and strategies for raising student achievement*. Alexandria, VA: Association for Supervision and Curriculum Development.

Tovani, C. (2000). *I read it, but I don't get it: Comprehension strategies for adolescent readers*. Portland, ME: Stenhouse Publishers.

Weiderhold, C. (1995). Cooperative learning and higher level thinking: The Q-Matrix. San Clemente, CA: Kagan.

Williamson, R., & Blackburn, B. (2010). *Rigorous schools and classrooms: Leading the way*. Larchmont, NY: Eye On Education.

Wormeli, R. (2006). *Fair isn't always equal: Assessing and grading in the differentiated classroom*. Portland, ME: Stenhouse Publishing.

Notes

Notes

Notes

Notes